THE Smarter PHYSICIAN

INVESTING IN YOUR PERSONAL FINANCIAL HEALTH

Bhagwan Satiani, MD, MBA, FACS

Medical Group Management Association (MGMA) publications are intended to provide current and accurate information and are designed to assist readers in becoming more familiar with the subject matter covered. Such publications are distributed with the understanding that MGMA does not render any legal, accounting, or other professional advice that may be construed as specifically applicable to an individual situation. No representations or warranties are made concerning the application of legal or other principles discussed by the authors to any specific factual situation, nor is any prediction made concerning how any particular judge, government official, or other person will interpret or apply such principles. Specific factual situations should be discussed with professional advisors.

Production Credits
Editorial Director: Marilee E. Aust
Project Editor: Anne Serrano, MA
Page Design, Composition, and Production: Glacier Publishing Services, Inc.
Copy Editor: Alys Novak, MBA, Discovery Communications
Proofreader: Glacier Publishing Services, Inc.
Cover Design: Ian Serff, Serff Creative Group, Inc.

MGMA Information Center Subcommittee
Chair: Charles D. Moses, FACMPE
Samantha Kempster, MBA, CMPE
Carolyn Pickles, MBA, FACMPE
Mary Pat Whaley, FACMPE

Library of Congress Cataloging-in-Publication Data
Satiani, Bhagwan.
   The smarter physician. Investing in your personal financial health / by Bhagwan Satiani.
      p. ; cm.
   Includes bibliographical references and index.
   Summary: "Topics discussed in the book - ranging from investments to insurance and estate planning and finally to retirement planning - require close attention, even from busy physicians. It can be used by practice administrators to help their physicians get on the track to personal financial freedom"--Provided by publisher.
   ISBN 978-1-56829-287-8
   1. Physicians--Finance, Personal. I. Medical Group Management Association. II. Title. III. Title: Investing in your personal financial health.
   [DNLM: 1. Practice Management, Medical--economics. 2. Economics. W 80 S253s 2007]
   R728.5.S2483 2007
   610.68'1--dc22
                                                                                            2007020116

Item #6800
ISBN: 978-1-56829-287-8

Copyright © 2007 Medical Group Management Association

Printed in the United States of America
10 9 8 7 6 5 4 3 2 1

The Smarter Physician Series

Volume 1
Demystifying the Business of Medicine in Your Practice

Volume 2
Conquering Your Practice's Billing and Reimbursement

Volume 3
Investing in Your Personal Financial Health

Dedication

I am eternally grateful to God for linking my life to this great country, the United States of America. My ever-lasting gratitude goes to my parents, Sobhraj and Lachmi Satiani, for the foundation of patience, self-reliance, and trust in God. My children, Anmol, Anand, and Nidhi, deserve a special thank you for their constant doting love, support, and encouragement. Finally, I am blessed to have the ideal friend, wife, and companion for more than 36 years who has been a pillar of strength and given me the freedom to indulge and follow my dreams. Thank you, Mira.

Acknowledgments

I am very grateful to all the contributing authors for the hard work in writing their chapters on time and responding to many requests for clarification. Their expertise and real-world experience has added immensely to this work. Many individuals helped in many ways during the process of writing the three volumes in The Smarter Physician Series. My sincere thanks to: Anmol Satiani and Anand Satiani for proofreading and insightful comments; Todd Wheeler for a helpful critique of the chapter on compensation; Chris Kaiser and Ray Manley for help with use of relative value units and department policies; Steve LeClair and Howard Pirwitz with UBS for generous assistance with several chapters on finance; to Charlie Black, Lee Miller, and Ron Ohsner with HRH for their insights into professional liability insurance; to Nate Goldberg for suggesting changes in the chapters on life and disability insurance; to Tim Nagy for a review of the tax status of hospitals; to Chester Krisiewicz and Loribeth Bethel for advice on taxation topics; to Asim Sheikh with UBS for his critique of chapters on stocks, mutual funds, and bonds; and Phil Heit for educating me on book publishing. I would like to thank my friend and colleague, Pat Vaccaro (Division of Vascular Surgery), and Chris Ellison (department chair), for their support as well as Wiley "Chip" Souba, our dean at The Ohio State University College of Medicine for encouraging me and promptly agreeing to write a chapter. Finally, my gratitude to a very hard-working, patient editor assigned by MGMA: Bob Redling. Thank you, Bob.

Also appreciated is the assistance from MGMA's Information Center staff including Marilee Aust, Editorial Director; Anne Serrano, Information Products Manager; and Alys Novak, copy editor.

Contents

List of Tables

List of Figures

Introduction

Generations of physicians have practiced medicine with pride and have been able to maintain a disconnect between the economic and the clinical aspects of medicine. Some practitioners continue to insist that the practice of medicine is simply healing the sick and that the business side will take care of itself.

That may have been true in years past. The fact is, being better versed in the economic side of medicine and providing the best and most compassionate care are not mutually exclusive. The two are perfectly compatible. Indeed, in this era, the physician must make good business decisions in order to provide uncompensated care that is part of all physicians' responsibility to society. Even a decade ago, operating margins were generous enough to allow physicians to be inattentive to the business side of the practice and still be able to make a good living, provide charity care, give office staff well-deserved benefits, and pay malpractice premiums. Not any more.

The Accreditation Council for Graduate Medical Education (ACGME), which is responsible for the accreditation of post-medical school training in the United States, has issued a new initiative called "Educating Physicians for the 21st Century" that recognizes the importance of addressing a serious deficiency in training programs.[1] The ACGME has identified six general competencies for medical residency programs, one of which is "Systems-Based Practice." This competency calls for educating residents in the economics of health care systems, billing, coding, and patient safety.[2]

As the senior physician in my practice, I was expected to know everything ranging from office hiring procedures to personal finance in guiding junior associates. With no background in the economic side of medicine and a 20-something secretary with no business or management experience, I believe I have made every mistake managing a practice that is possible—and survived!

Physicians are taught little to nothing in medical school or their residency about the non-clinical aspect of medicine. (See Table I.1 for a review of the knowledge base needed for accomplishing tasks during a medical career.) Basic information about how and where to look for a successful practice,

Table I.1   Knowledge Base Needed for Accomplishing Tasks During a Medical Career

Career Stages	Task	Knowledge Needed
Residency	Attending presence for services, E&M codes	Billing/coding/fraud and abuse
	Dealing with pharmaceutical companies/vendors	Ethical guidelines
	Dealing with mal-occurrences in patient care	Malpractice, litigation
	Looking for a job	Contract negotiations
	Assessing a buy-in	Valuation of practice
	Interviewing, negotiating signing bonus, moving expenses	Anti-kickback regulations, fraud and abuse regulations, compensation
Practice	Starting practice	Basic accounting/finance/corporations/tax structure, payment systems
	Hiring/firing staff	Human resources
	Pursuing academic practice	Stark laws relating to academic medical centers, practice plans, contract negotiations
	Having a successful practice	Marketing, cost–volume–profit analysis, budgets, financial ratios
	Ensuring professional liability understood	Medico-legal knowledge, professional liability insurance, National Practitioner Data Bank, expert witness role
	Ensuring health, disability/life insurance issues covered	Health/disability/life insurance
	Saving for children's education	Forms of trusts, educational savings account
	Having a pension plan	Regulations, retirement plans
	Performing as a hospital director	Structure of not-for-profits, Stark/anti-kickback regulations, physician–hospital relations
	Leasing space from hospital, leasing space to hospital and others	Anti-kickback regulations, Stark laws
	Investing	Finance, stocks/bonds/fixed investments, taxable and non-taxable investments, trusts, savings programs
	Opening outpatient facility	Joint ventures, accounting, finance, Stark law
	Helping hospital with efficiency program	Gainsharing, pay-for-performance programs
	Billing	Reimbursement issues, Medicare, private insurers, mechanics of billing/coding/ revenue cycle/False Claims Act
End of practice	Selling practice	Valuation of practice
	Retiring	Retirement planning, Medicare
	Becoming a physician executive, looking for part-time employment	Physician–executive transformation, contract negotiations, business schools

©2007 Satiani

what to ask in an interview, how to spot problems in an employment opportunity, and be aware of the value of the financial package being offered (other than the salary) is woefully inadequate. Any useful information from other residents is mixed with either outdated or inaccurate data so as to render it less than valuable. New physicians are then expected to start by hiring the most valuable commodity in a practice: a good business manager. The expectation is that they will match their skill in patient care with being financially successful. In an era of group practices, they rely on their senior colleagues to manage the business side. The likelihood that the senior colleagues have any formal education or training in this area is slim. All decisions are based on personal experience, "we have always done it this way," or total reliance on advice from their accountants, attorneys, and financial advisors. By the time a junior physician discovers that he/she made a mistake understanding what was really in the contract, that the balance sheet of the hiring entity was a disaster, the retirement plan was inadequate, the financial advisor was not honest, and that the billing practices were illegal, valuable time has been wasted.

The urge to learn and then teach younger physicians about the business side of medicine made me realize that there was room for a resource that physicians could refer to and read about basic business topics valuable in a medical practice. This book started out as a small manual for residents, to be given out as reference material in business/practice management classes. The current form has been made possible by all the contributors who have labored over their assignments with no expectation other than to help with the education process of the all-important business managers for existing practices, future physicians, and current practitioners who desire to gain enough knowledge to ask the right questions of their professional advisors. It is my hope that this book serves as a stimulus to learn much more than the small slice of knowledge that this book offers. Undoubtedly, there will be mistakes and omissions that come with a first attempt at organizing a project such as this.

In the natural cycle of one's career, the topics discussed in this third volume of The Smarter Physician series—ranging from investments to insurances and estate planning and, finally, to retirement planning—all require close attention even from busy physicians. The chapters are not about "how to do it" or which stocks or funds to pick. Rather, this volume hopes to provide the ingredients for critical analysis of the information presented to busy practitioners, before they commit their hard-earned assets. Chapter 1 ("Setting Your Course: How to Take Charge of the Financial Planning Process") sets the tone by engaging in a general discussion about the financial planning process and qualifications of financial advisors. Chapter 2 ("Investments: What You Need to Know About Stocks and Mutual Funds"), which is enriched by the experience of financial management advisor and author John E. Sestina, CFP, ChFC, and chapter 3 ("Investing in Bonds and Other Fixed-Income Instruments) inform the reader about risk measurement, benchmarks, diversification, and fee structures of equities and bonds. Chapter 4 ("Do Your Assets Correlate?") gets you started reviewing your assets and how they correlate with each other.

A long-term vision requires close attention to compensation benefits that are covered in each subsequent chapter of this volume, including retirement plans of various kinds (Chapter 5: Planning for Retirement) and life insurance (Chapter 6: Life Insurance: Tips for Buying It and Using It). Chapter 7 ("Estate Planning Essentials: Protecting Your Family and Your Legacy") was written by attorney Scot C. Crow, JD, LLM, CFP, to cover the essentials of this important aspect of planning. Disability insurance is covered in chapter 8 ("Disability Insurance: Protect Your Income When Illness or Injury Occurs"). Saving for higher education starts early, and chapter 9 ("Saving for Higher Education Expenses") clarifies all of the choices currently available.

Finally, as many physicians tend to be compulsive individuals, they find that balancing a full-time academic or private practice with family commitments is difficult and stressful. Chapter 10 ("Managing Your Time, Your Career, and Your Life") was written to provide a larger perspective based on 30 years of medical practice and learning some important lessons in life.

As an extra value, the book contains a CD with additional material, including a glossary and a list of financial information and health care law Websites, as well as other valuable resources.

References

1. Accreditation Council for Graduate Medical Education, www.acgme.org (accessed May 23, 2006).

2. B. Joyce, "Introduction to Competency-based Education, Facilitator's Guide" ACGME (April 2006) www.acgme.org/outcome/e-learn/21M1_facmanual.pdf (accessed May 23, 2006).

Chapter 1

Setting Your Course: How to Take Charge of the Financial Planning Process

During your career as a physician you will face many new personal and professional challenges. Unfortunately, college and medical school do not teach young doctors how to confront, let alone conquer, the personal financial challenges they are about to face. However, financial planning does not have to be a mystery to you. By recognizing financial challenges and putting together an action plan, you can achieve your goals. This chapter introduces the challenges and the steps you can take to implement a proper financial plan.

Financial Challenges

Living Longer in Retirement

According to the U.S. Department of Health and Human Services, the median life expectancy for a 65-year-old male in United States is another 16.6 years; for a 65-year-old female it is another 19.5 years.[1] However, most Americans still want to retire in their early 60s. This presents a real challenge for financial planning because it is probable that many people will spend more years in retirement than they spent saving for retirement. Longevity alone makes retirement goals difficult to achieve.

Inflation

In addition to longer life expectancies, inflation continues to erode your purchasing power. For example, roll back the clock to the year 1980 (Table 1.1), when a first-class postage stamp cost $0.15. As of May 2007, that stamp became $0.41. More alarming are housing and vehicle costs, which have more than tripled. Unfortunately for investors, interest rates paid on money market and traditional savings accounts are often lower than the rate of inflation. Therefore, parking money in these "safe" accounts is not a viable long-term solution to savings needs because purchasing power is lost.

Table 1.1   Cost Increases, 1980–2005

Item	1980	2005
First-class postage	$0.15	$0.39
Loaf of bread	$0.48	$1.48
Gallon of milk	$1.60	$3.49
Average new car	$7,600	$27,800
Average new house	$86,159	$264,000
College education*	$5,769	$12,127

  * Annual in-state tuition, fees, room and board; four-year public universities, 2005–2006.

Sources: T. Flanagan, "COLA Wars," Government Executive.com, www.govexec.com/dailyfed/0906/090806rp.htm (accessed March 5, 2007); The College Board, *Trends in College Pricing, 2005*, (Washington, D.C.: The College Board, 2005), www.collegeboard.com/prod_downloads/press/cost05/trends_college_pricing_05.pdf (accessed March 5, 2007).

Social Security

You don't have to follow the news to know that problems exist in the Social Security system; all you have to do is read your yearly benefit statement. In 1950, the worker-to-beneficiary ratio was 16.5-to-1. Today, the worker-to-beneficiary ratio is 3.3-to-1. Within 40 years, the ratio drops to 2-to-1.[2] These figures make it easy to understand how Social Security was able to support retirees in 1950 with an income supplement for retirement. But due to a major demographic shift in our country in which fewer workers support benefit recipients, the Social Security Trust will be depleted in the year 2041. If change does not happen prior to 2041, benefits will be cut by 26 percent in 2042 with subsequent cuts in the following years. With this in mind, Social Security is not a reliable retirement income source. Therefore, prudent investors must establish alternative sources for retirement income.

Starting the Planning Process

Given these facts, you can see why financial planning is necessary. By planning early, you dramatically increase the likelihood of realizing your financial goals because you have the power of time and compounding on your side. Time gives you flexibility and options in the types of risks you can take. Furthermore, time allows compounding to work its magic on your investments (See chapter 7, Using Financial Statements to Make Decisions, in Volume 2 of The Smarter Physician Series [©2007 Medical Group Management Association] for details about compounding). Take a look at this example:

> Dr. Bob invests $100 per month for 20 years at 8 percent. At the end of 20 years his $24,000 investment is worth $59,295. If Dr. Bob

waited 10 years and still needed a portfolio valued at $59,295, he would have to save $322 per month at 8 percent for a total investment of $38,640. By waiting 10 years, Bob had to invest an additional $14,640.

As you can see, planning early guards against outliving your money and allows you to take charge of your financial destiny. So how do you begin the financial planning process? Start by answering four questions:

- What do I want out of life?

- What do I own, and what do I owe?

- What roads am I willing to take to reach my goals?

- Where do I go from here?

Although these questions seem elementary, the answers are critical because the best financial plan is the one that coordinates your values, investments, and time horizon into a cohesive strategy.

What Do I Want Out of Life?

Because we are all different and unique, we have different answers to this question. Some people want to travel while others want to volunteer their time. But no matter who we are, we all have one wish in common—maintaining our lifestyle. When answering this question, you need to really analyze yourself and your family. What are your core values? What motivates you to get out of bed in the morning? Only you can answer this question. When you do, you are ready to move on to the next step in financial planning.

What Do I Own, and What Do I Owe?

For many of us, finances are like the "junk drawer" in our home. We all have junk drawers, so take a moment to think about yours. You will find that this drawer is a collection of stuff you have gathered over time and stored in an unorganized fashion. When you put something in your junk drawer, you do so because you think that you may need it in the future.

Alarmingly, most of people treat their finances like their junk drawer. They fill this drawer with stuff such as:

- 401(k)s;

- Stocks;

- Bonds; and

- Life insurance.

Over time, people make several investment decisions and file them away in their financial junk drawer. If someone were to ask why you own the investments you do, and if they are part of a coordinated strategy, would you know how to answer the question?

Therefore, the second step of financial planning involves cracking open your financial junk drawer and taking an inventory. There are several good computer software programs on the market today that can help you with this step. Microsoft® Money and Quicken™ are two of the most popular programs. These programs guide you with step-by-step instructions for organizing your finances. Additionally, they help you develop a budget and track your expenses. This is important because you want to see how you utilize your money and determine if you spend it wisely. Once you are finished taking inventory, you can move onto the third element: how to coordinate your investments into an appropriate financial plan.

What Roads Am I Willing to Take to Reach My Financial Goals?

Most Americans spend more time every year planning their vacation than they do their finances. Assuming you are similar to your fellow Americans, think about how you plan your vacations.

If you decide to take a road trip, you don't just hop in your car and drive. Instead, you look at a Website such as www.mapquest.com or pull out the atlas and choose a destination. After settling on a destination, you pick the roads you will take based upon how quickly you want to get there. If your goal is to reach your destination as soon as possible, you will probably take the interstate. On the other hand, if your road trip is going to be an adventure, you will probably take back roads. The difference between the interstate and back roads is the time and risks involved. While the interstate is faster, accidents are often more devastating than those on the back roads.

With this in mind, the financial planning process is very similar to the vacation planning process. First, you establish your goals, and second, you determine how quickly you want to achieve your goals. It is best to look at each of your goals individually rather than collectively. If the goal is in the near term, you are probably risk averse. These goals are like driving on the back roads. On the other hand, if your goal is further in the future, you are probably more risk tolerant. In this case the interstate may be more appropriate.

Risk is a personal decision and not necessarily age-related. Risk is the amount of loss an individual is willing to inure. While it is true that younger people have more time to recover from financial loss, the fact remains that many young people are not willing to take high risks with their money. At the same time, there are many older people willing to take very large risks with their money. You need to decide for yourself what types of risks you are willing to take. If you are young and decide that you do not want to take large risks, that is fine. Just realize that it may take you longer to achieve your goals.

You may have different risk tolerances for your different goals. For example, you may be conservative with your emergency funds and aggressive with your retirement funds. By maintaining separate accounts for your different goals, you are better suited for managing the risk across your investments more appropriately. Additionally, separate accounts allow you to benchmark and measure your progress. You will learn more about this topic when you answer the fourth question of financial planning.

Where Do I Go from Here?

In deciding what investments to make, it is useful to first consider what they will be used for. Investments can be broken down into four general uses:

- Emergencies;
- Retirement;
- Financial goals other than retirement; and
- Insurance.

Emergency funds are used for just that, emergencies. Dinners out and vacations are not considered emergencies, so you should keep these funds separate from your checking account. Additionally, funding this account should be a top priority, and the money should be kept readily accessible in a bank or money market account.

Most financial planners suggest that single-income households should set aside funds to cover expenses for six months. Dual-income households should plan to save enough to cover expenses for three months.

A new school of thought on emergency funds suggests using home equity lines of credit, rather than setting aside money in a bank account. While home equity is a viable source for quick money, this is a risky strategy. If your income shortfall lasts longer than expected, you are putting yourself at risk of losing your home. Therefore, it is more advisable to fund a bank account rather than opening a home equity line of credit.

Once your emergency fund is established, you should move on to your financial priorities. Funding your retirement should be a top priority. Although you may want to pay for your child's college or wedding, the fact remains that you may live for 20 to 30 years in retirement. That is a long time to go without a paycheck. Therefore, you need to get in the habit early in your career of making regular contributions to your retirement plan. By establishing your retirement plan early in your career, you may be able to contribute less and take fewer risks. This makes realizing retirement in your early 60s more probable.

While it is true that you can borrow against your 401(k) and take money out of your IRA to make a down payment on a home or pay for educational expenses, this is not the purpose of the account. Your retirement account should always be viewed as the account of last resort. Other accounts should be used before taking money out of your retirement plan.

The third component of investments is for financial goals other than retirement. These goals may include college funds, weddings, second homes, or whatever else you may want in life. As stated earlier, these goals should be funded *after* your emergency fund and retirement plan are funded. However, how you prioritize your goals is up to you and ultimately should reflect your core values.

Using Diversification to Reduce Risk

Investment risk is managed by diversifying money across a broad range of stocks and bonds. What is diversification? The easiest way to understand diversification is by thinking of a traffic jam. When you get stuck in a traffic jam, it always seems that your lane comes to a stop while the lane beside you continues to move ahead. Without much thought, most drivers shift to the moving lane. Unfortunately, once they change lanes, the new lane comes to a stop and their prior lane is now pulling ahead. Diversification is like having a car in every lane on the highway. It doesn't matter which lane is moving forward and which lane is stopped because you are always making progress toward your goal.

Sadly, most investors change investments in the same way they change lanes in a traffic jam. Investors always want in on the hot investment, but like the traffic jam, most investors get into the investment too late to achieve any benefit. Dalbar, a company that measures investor satisfaction, supports this in a study from 1984 to 2002. During this period, the S&P 500 averaged 12.22 percent, while the average mutual-fund investor averaged 2.57 percent.[3] Had average investors properly diversified their investments and maintained their original strategy, they would have realized a greater return.

However, diversification is not the S&P 500 alone. Investors have to own a small piece of a variety of investments such as large stocks, small stocks, international stocks, and bonds. This is referred to as *asset allocation*. By further broadening your investment exposure, you lower your risk and take the volatility out of your account balances. This puts you on the right road for realizing your financial goals.

Using Insurance to Manage Risk

Insurance coverage is another critical component of investing. Like asset allocation and diversification, insurance is the process of risk management. You are your most valuable asset, and the most effective way you make money is by practicing your profession. Therefore, you should carry the appropriate level of insurance on your health and life.

Health insurance can be broken down into three categories: medical care, disability, and long-term care. While you are probably familiar with health insurance, you may not be so familiar with disability and long-term care insurance. Disability insurance ensures your income in the event you are unable to work for an extended period of time. Unfortunately, many individuals turn down disability insurance coverage because of the high premium costs. However, statistics show that only 13 percent of disabilities are because of accidents. The remaining 87 percent are the result of illness.[4] With this in mind, disability insurance is as important as your medical insurance. (See chapter 8 for an in-depth explanation of how to select disability-insurance coverage.)

Long-term care insurance is something most young people do not think about because this insurance is used for nursing home and home health care. However, be aware that the earlier you buy the insurance, the less expensive the premiums are. It is advised that individuals should look into purchasing the insurance while in their mid-forties. During this period of life the premiums are reasonable.

Life Insurance

Next to your emergency fund and health insurance, life insurance should be a top priority, especially if you have dependents. Most individuals underestimate the appropriate level of life-insurance coverage, so a good starting point is insuring seven times your annual income. However, refer back to the first question of financial planning and your core values. The appropriate coverage level comes down to your financial goals. For example, a married individual with young children may feel it is necessary to carry more coverage than a single person with no dependents.

In addition to choosing the appropriate level of coverage, it is important that you choose the right type of life insurance policy. There are three main types of life insurance policies: whole life, universal life, and term life. These types of coverage are discussed in more depth in chapter 6. In summary, whole life insurance is a permanent insurance policy that has a guaranteed death benefit and guaranteed premium for the life of the insured. Additionally, whole life insurance has a guaranteed savings component called *cash value*. The contract owner can borrow against the cash value tax free. However, whole life insurance is the most expensive form of life insurance.

Universal life insurance is also a permanent insurance policy with more flexibility than whole life insurance. Like whole life, universal life has a death benefit and cash value. Unlike whole life, universal life is sold on the basis of interest rate or stock market assumptions. This means that the premiums of universal life insurance are not guaranteed. Contract owners may have to increase their premium payments if interest rates or the stock market is depressed. Although universal life insurance is less expensive than whole life, the contract owner assumes more risk.

Lastly, term life insurance is not a permanent insurance policy and does not accumulate cash value. As the name implies, term insurance provides protection only for a determined period of time such as 10 or 20 years. Due to the short period of coverage and the absence of cash value, term insurance is a very economical way of acquiring a large amount of insurance without high premiums.

Many families find that their insurance needs resemble a bell curve. While there is always some need of life insurance during the course of a lifetime, the highest need is often during the child-raising years. Term insurance may be most suitable for insuring the child-raising years, while permanent insurance ensures the base coverage always needed throughout your lifetime. Once again, refer back to your answer regarding core values. This will help you properly construct the appropriate life insurance coverage.

Create the Plan   Financial planning is not a one-time event. Rather, financial planning is an ongoing process and the plan itself becomes a living, breathing document that is updated and assessed throughout your life. Most important, the plan allows you to track your progress toward your goals. By establishing benchmarks, you will be able to see whether you are on pace to reach your goals. You will naturally find that in some years you are ahead of pace and may reach your goals quicker than expected. On the other hand, there will be years when you are not on track to reach your goals on time. Both scenarios require retrospect and examination of your investments. Because the financial markets are volatile, you need to continually reassess the risks you are taking and compare them to the risks you are willing to take.

It is important that you track your investments quarterly and review your plan annually. Quarterly you may find it necessary to rebalance your investments. Rebalancing means adjusting your investments back to your original mix of stocks and bonds. Although it may seem counterproductive to sell your better performers and reinvest the gains into categories that may not be performing well, you are lowering your risk and taking the volatility out of your portfolio. Annually, you should review the plan to determine if the plan is still materially relevant for your goals.

Getting Advice

At this point you can tell that financial planning and investment management is a full-time job. Due to time constraints and possibly the lack of desire to take on the task of managing your investments, you may decide that you want to work with a financial professional. While there is a plethora of financial advisors, choosing an advisor doesn't have to be a daunting task.

Due to regulatory changes in the financial services industry, the difference between financial service firms has blurred. Therefore, your focus should be on the client–advisor relationship. While it is true you want to work with a firm you believe can offer the products and services you need, you should be looking for an advisor with interests aligned with your own. The advisor's wealth management approach should be similar to how you want your financial plan managed. This relationship is more important than the firm the advisor works for or whether the advisor charges commissions or fees.

As you may already know, finding an advisor willing to work with you is not a difficult task. Due to your profession, advisors will be seeking you out. Proceed with caution before committing to a financial advisor. You may want to survey your coworkers and ask them for a referral. If you want to find an advisor on your own, here are steps for finding the right person.

The first step involves the interview. The purpose of this interview is for both parties to determine if the other party is a fit for how they want to do business. Some questions you may want to ask the advisor are:

- What is your investment philosophy?

- Why are you qualified to watch my money?

- Do you use market timing?

- Does portfolio size matter?

- How do you arrive at exact fees charged?

  – Do you charge commissions?

  – Are you a fee-only planner?

  – Do you assess a fee based on assets under management?

- How will you track my money and report progress?

- Where did you receive your formal education and what was your major?

- In addition to your formal education, have you gone on to receive any other designations such as certified public accountant (CPA), certified financial planner (CFP), chartered financial analyst (CFA), or certified life underwriter (CLU)? If so, what does this designation mean?

- Have you had a formal complaint filed against you?

Because all advisors run their businesses differently, there is not a standard set of questions you should expect them to ask you. However, be prepared for them to talk to you about your experience with investing, feelings about money, your goals, and your income.

Once the interview is complete and you feel comfortable with the advisor, you can check out their background and credentials. All financial professionals who provide either advice or investment products are required to register with a regulatory authority. Advisors who charge commissions or fees for managing your assets are required to be licensed and registered with the National Association of Securities Dealers (NASD). The NASD maintains a database of registered representatives' employment backgrounds for the past 10 years. This database can be accessed over the Internet at www.nasd.org. In addition to employment backgrounds, you can see if any formal complaints have been filed against the advisor.

Some advisors are financial planners who only get paid to write the financial plan and implement the investment through another firm. In this case they are registered investment advisors and are required to be registered as such with their state's security commission. Additionally, they may be required to be registered with the Securities and Exchange Commission (SEC). Registered investment advisors are mandated to provide you with a brochure that includes their background information. This brochure, referred to as the ADV-II, is filed annually with their state security commission.

While it would be wonderful to believe that all advisors are looking out for your best interests, unfortunately this is not always true. Beware of advisors putting pressure on you with phrases such as "beat the market," "guaranteed," "you need to hurry," "exclusive," and "you can't lose." Remember, this is your money. You have to feel that the advisor is always looking out for your interests first.

Sources of Financial Advice

Most investment advisors and brokers are honest and do the best they can for their clients. However, some succumb to the temptation to pad their incomes by selling products that do not benefit the client but generate income for themselves. The brokerage industry has taken steps to change the perception that financial advisors do not put their clients' interests ahead of their own. Some firms, such as Morgan Stanley, offer financial planning and advice for a fee, while the actual transaction is executed by another firm of the client's choice. However, as Opdyke and Wei[5] point out, offering yet another set of choices makes the investor more confused about what kind of advisor to choose for a particular transaction. They have divided the categories into the following three main choices according to the task.

Stockbrokers (Registered Representatives)

- May be brokerage-based or independent;
- Are regulated by the Securities Act of 1934 and by the NASD, which is the primary non-governmental self-regulatory agency of the U.S. securities industry;
- Receive commissions related to type of product sold. Alternately may receive an annual fixed or negotiated fee based on the total assets being managed. The investment firm in return is guaranteed a certain percentage of assets and a steady income stream, which can add up to significant dollars in large retirement accounts. Regardless of how the account performs, the firm receives a fee every quarter;
- May offer "wrap accounts" in which a flat percentage is charged on total assets under management with no separate charges for trades. This arrangement removes the incentive for the firm to execute more trades than necessary. Separately managed accounts allow an investor to directly own stocks or bonds for total fixed fees (including consultation, trading, and management) that appear as a line item on a

Table 1.2   Brokerage and Advisory Accounts Compared

Brokerage Account	Advisory Account
Non-discretionary (Broker cannot execute trades without your prior permission.)	Discretionary (Broker has authority to trade without prior permission.)
Prime purpose is the business of trading stocks and other securities and any advice offered is solely incidental.	A separate fee for advice is paid to the broker.
All documents (statements, advertising, marketing, etc.) clearly indicate it is a brokerage, not an advisory account.	The broker (advisor) presents his/her services as a financial planner.

Sources: U.S. Securities and Exchange Commission, www.sec.gov/investor/brokers.htm (accessed 3/8/2006) and NASD, http://apps.nasd.com/datadirectory/nasd/prodesignations.aspx.

statement. The usual practice is that a quarterly fee is fixed to a percentage of assets; the percentage charged may decline as the amount invested increases. Generally, fees for wrap accounts range from 1 percent to 2 percent. One must be careful to check whether there are mutual fund fees or other recurring expenses in addition to these "fee-only" charges. Those additional fees may increase the total cost to 2 percent or 3 percent of the portfolio. If so, the net return to the investor minus the 3 percent cost might, after inflation, end up less than from a balanced, unmanaged stock and bond portfolio; and

- May provide clients a financial plan, but only as part of an advisory relationship according to SEC rules (see Table 1.2). Under the so-called Merrill Lynch rule, fee-based advisors and brokerages do not have a fiduciary responsibility to act in the client's best interest, but instead are allowed to operate under "suitability" guidelines. That is, they are only required to recommend reasonable choices to their clients. However, a recent U.S. Court of Appeals decision has over-turned the SEC rule exempting brokerage firms that charge asset-based fees from investment advisory regulations under specified conditions.

If you don't need advice on financial planning but simply want someone to trade securities for you, then consider the services of a broker. In addition to full-service brokers, there are discount firms such as Charles Schwab, Ameriprise, and others that provide most of their services online to keep costs and fees down. These firms tend to feature lower transaction fees, but offer many of the other services provided by brokers. In light of this competition, many traditional brokers have morphed into financial advisors or financial planners.

When dealing with advisors or brokers who charge fees, keep in mind those fees are negotiable. This is especially true as the amount invested grows larger, or if you have several accounts with the firm.

Financial Advisors (or Registered Investment Advisors)

- May be brokerage-based or independent (registered investment advisor);

- Focus on overall financial planning rather than buying and selling individual stocks or funds;

- Are regulated by the SEC under the rules of the Investment Advisers Act of 1940, which was passed by Congress to regulate all aspects of securities. Generally, financial advisers who manage $25 million or more in client assets generally must register with the SEC; those managing less than this amount are registered with the state. The SEC is empowered by Congress to regulate all aspects of securities;

- May have less of an incentive to sell in-house funds, although investment firms may provide advisors with extra incentives to sell their products; and

- Offer advice and execute transactions ranging from life insurance to retirement planning.

Financial Planners

- May be brokerage-based or independent;

- May be both financial advisors and also financial planners and are regulated by the SEC;

- Provide short- and long-term comprehensive financial planning;

- Are strictly fee-based. Consultation and analysis fees will vary depending on the size and variety of assets and the tasks performed. Average fees start at about $2,000;

- May offer brokerage-type services. Clients can trade stocks and other securities;

- May charge a one-time fee to develop the plan; and

- Offer advice, but have no direct ties to investment or brokerage firms.

If you feel you know what securities you want to buy or sell, you may want to hire a financial planner to look at the entire picture of your holdings. The planner also can advise you on the tax implications and future growth of your investments, as well as other matters including succession planning.

Risk management also involves working with an estate-planning attorney. Your attorney will walk you through the steps of properly titling your assets and protecting them in our litigious society. Additionally, estate-planning attorneys can draft wills, guardianships, and powers of attorney that express your wishes in the event of your death or incapacity to handle your own financial affairs. See chapter 7 for a discussion of estate planning.

Conclusion

Throughout this chapter you can see that the financial planning process is necessary because financial burdens will continue to be placed upon your shoulders throughout your lifetime. However, most people make the financial planning process more complex than it needs to be. Fortunately, you now know that financial planning can be accomplished by answering four questions:

- What do I want out of life?

- What do I own, and what do I owe?

- What roads am I willing to take to reach my financial goals?

- Where do I go from here?

By referring to these four questions when you are faced with a new financial challenge, you are bettered armed to make informed decisions and properly implement those decisions into your cohesive financial plan.

References

1. National Center for Health Statistics, "Health, United States, 2004," Centers for Disease Control and Prevention, www.cdc.gov/nchs/data/hus/hus04trend.pdf#027 (accessed July 25, 2006).

2. Social Security Administration, "Frequently Asked Questions About Social Security's Future," www.socialsecurity.gov/qa.htm (accessed July 25, 2006).

3. Dalbar, Inc., "Market Chasing Mutual Fund Investors Earn Less than Inflation," July 15, 2003, www.dalbarinc.com/content/showpage.asp?page=2003071601&r=/pressroom/default.asp&s=Return+To+Press+Releases (accessed July 25, 2006).

4. National Institute on Disability and Rehabilitation Research, "Disability in the United States Prevalence and Causes, 1992," www.eric.ed.gov.

5. J. Opdyke and L. Wei, "Stockbrokers Loosen Up Their Ties." *Wall Street J*, April 29–30 (2006): B1.

Additional Resources

Certified Financial Planner—www.cpf.com

Fee-Only Financial Planners—www.feeonly.org or wwwgarrettplanning-network.com

Financial Planning Association—www.fpanet.org

National Association of Personal Financial Advisors—www.napfa.org

Chapter 2

Investments: What You Need to Know About Stocks and Mutual Funds

John E. Sestina, CFP, ChFC, and Bhagwan Satiani, MD, MBA, FACS

Simply put, investing is the process of putting away money for future use. Technically, you might say, sticking your money beneath your mattress is an investment. However, it produces no interest and is prone to fire and theft. In today's society, with all the options available, a bank account may be the equivalent of the mattress at home. When money is placed in a bank account, it is not prone to theft and fire, but earns very little income and loses buying power.

The three basic building blocks of investing are: cash equivalents (investments such as cash, bank accounts, and money markets) that you can convert quickly into cash; stocks (or mutual funds, which can have a variety of investments); and fixed-income investments (for example, U.S. Treasury bonds). Fixed-income investments are discussed in chapter 3.

There comes a time when every company needs to raise capital, whether to establish a satellite office, expand the business, or develop and sell a new product. Small businesses can usually generate these funds by borrowing money from a bank. Larger businesses borrow money, or raise it from investors by selling them a part of the company via shares of stock.

The Stock Market

When you buy a share of stock, you are a partial owner in the company with a claim on every asset and every penny of earnings—however small that claim may be. Of course, most stock buyers do not think like owners, and it is not as if they have a booming voice in the actual operation of the company in which they own stock. The ownership structure of the company is what gives a stock its value. Stock certificates would be worth just the paper they are printed on if shareholders did not have a claim on earnings. When a company's earnings improve, investors are willing to

Figure 2.1   Stock and Bond Returns over Time

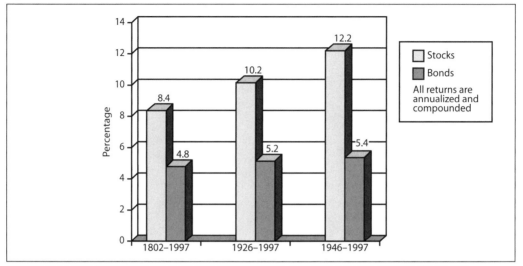

Source: J.J. Siegel, *Stocks for the Long Run*, 2nd ed. New York: McGraw-Hill (1998): 13, 15. Reproduced with permission of McGraw Hill.

pay more for the stock. The price of a stock is different than the value of the company in which the investor is buying the stock.

Market capitalization is a measure of the value of a company. This is the stock price multiplied by the number of shares outstanding. *Stock price*, on the other hand, is the cost of capital and future earnings depending on the time value of money. The stock price, therefore, is more indicative of future growth of the company, not the current value of the company. Domestic (U.S.) stocks are for the most part traded on the New York Stock Exchange (NYSE), the National Association of Securities Dealers Automated Quotation (NASDAQ), and the American Stock Exchange (AMEX).

Traditionally, over a period of time, stocks have been strong investments. In many cases, as the economy grows, so do corporate earnings and thus stock prices. Since the 1920s, the average large company stock has provided more than a 10 percent return per year (Figure 2.1). In the 80-year period between 1926 and 2005, stocks generated higher returns than bonds in 49 of those years. This is a much better return than a U.S. Savings Bond or a savings account at your local bank. Of course, as any stock investor knows, prolonged bear markets can decimate a portfolio. Since World War II, Wall Street has endured a dozen *bear markets*, which are defined as a sustained decline of about 20 percent in the value of the major market indices such as the Dow Jones Industrial Average (DJIA). One of the sharpest and longest in history began in March 2000 and ended in the fall of 2002. Bull markets eventually follow these downturns, yet the prospect of an eventual end to the downturn offers little comfort to investors in the midst of the downdraft. A *correction* in the market is said to occur in the form of a short decline in prices (between 10 percent and 20 percent in the value of a major stock index), which happens after a period of rising stock prices.

You must remember that investing is a long-term endeavor. Therefore you must be able to endure the potential anguish of a bear market to enjoy the fruits of a bull market.

Classification of Stocks

There are thousands of stocks to choose from, so investors usually like to classify stocks into different categories.

The usual type of stock owned by investors is called a *common* stock. Shares of common stock give the investor ownership of part of the company, a vote to elect board members, and a claim against any profits such as dividends. Owners of what is called a *preferred* stock do not have the same rights as owners of common stock. These investors get a guaranteed dividend (referring to debt obligations of the company, such as bonds) in contrast to common-stock shareholders whose dividends are variable.

Large vs. Small "Cap"

A company's size reflects its *market capitalization* (*cap*), which is described as the current share price times the total number of shares outstanding. There are three market capitalization divisions in the U.S. market: large cap (usually $5 billion and above), mid-cap (usually $1 billion to $5 billion), and small cap (usually less than $1 billion). Large-cap companies are usually established and stable. However, due to their size, they often have lower growth potential than small caps. In the long term, small-cap stocks tend to rise at a more rapid pace. It is much easier to expand revenues and earnings quickly when you start at $12 million, for example, than $12 billion. When profitability increases, stock prices follow. Of course, with their less-developed management structures, small-cap stocks are more likely to experience problems as they grow and pose incremental risk for investors.

Types of Risk

Risk tolerance and time frame are important factors when considering the choice of investments and diversification. There are two main types of risks. *Diversifiable risk* is the risk associated with an individual stock that

Table 2.1   Effects of Inflation, Declining Value of $1 Million

Years	Inflation Rate			
	2%	3%	4%	5%
5	$903,921	$858,734	$815,373	$773,781
10	$817,073	$737,424	$664,833	$598,737
15	$738,569	$633,251	$542,086	$463,291
20	$667,608	$543,794	$442,002	$358,486

can be eliminated by including it in a large portfolio, usually of at least 40 stocks. This type of risk is random and consists of events such as lawsuits. The risk can be reduced by diversification where bad events in one portion of the portfolio will be cancelled by positive developments in other portions of the portfolio. The other type of risk is called the *market risk*, which cannot be eliminated because it includes events such as war, recession, and inflation.

Inflation is the increasing price of goods and services with time. When looking at the long-term horizon, the effect of inflation on investment returns is very important. Because of inflation, your money loses some of its purchasing power over time (Table 2.1). Continuing inflation can compound into an extensive loss of value. Inflation is your fiercest enemy. It always has been, and always will be—even when the rate of inflation is low. An average annual inflation rate of 3 percent or 4 percent sounds insignificant, but over the course of 20 years an annual rate of 4-percent inflation would drive the value of a single dollar down to $0.44, causing:[1]

- A $0.39 postage stamp to almost double to $0.81;
- A $1,000 refrigerator to cost almost $2,200; and
- A $23,000 automobile to cost $50,000.

Going back to 1945, inflation has decreased the value of a dollar every year except 1949 and 1950. Inflation does more than make consumer goods cost more; it also reduces the return you receive on investments. Table 2.2 shows how inflation has cut into annual stock market returns.[2]

Regardless of what your portfolio contains, your investment goal should always be to beat inflation by at least 2 percent per year after taxes. This is called the *real return*. A *nominal return* is the return unadjusted for inflation. On paper, a 2-percent return doesn't sound dramatic, but if you achieve this, you will be a winner in the investment game. You may not

Table 2.2   Inflation's Impact on Stock Returns, 1802–1997

Time Period	Total Nominal Annual Return (unadjusted for inflation)	Average Annual Increase in Consumer Price Index	Total Real Annual Return (adjusted for inflation)
1802–1997	8.4%	1.3%	7%
1982–1997	16.7%	3.4%	12.8%

Source: J.M. Bogle, *Common Sense on Mutual Funds*, New York: J. Wiley & Sons (1999). Used with permission.

make a 2-percent real return every year. Some years you'll do better, and other years you'll do worse. Still, you should aim for a 2-percent average real return. The author (Sestina) has been a financial planner for many years and seen first-hand many times where people reach their investment goal by beating inflation by a modest amount.

Measurement of Risk

The long-term data show that although the stock market has generated fairly steady returns over the years, there have been periods of considerable variability, and therefore, risk for the investor. To quantify this risk, several measures are commonly utilized.

Standard Deviation

Standard deviation is a measure of the range of an investment's return or the scatter of a set of numbers over a period of time.[3] As John Bogle explains, if "an investment has earned an average annual return of 10 percent and two-thirds of its annual returns have ranged between –5 percent and +25 percent, a range of 15 percentage points in either direction, one standard deviation is defined as 15.[2] In other words, two-thirds of the time the yearly return of the asset will be between one standard deviation above and one standard deviation below the mean value.[3] As expected, the standard deviation is narrow for assets usually carrying a lower risk and larger for assets worth a greater risk. Bernstein has estimated the standard deviation of common investments as follows:[3]

- Cash: 2 percent to 3 percent;
- Bonds: 3 percent to 5 percent;
- Conservative domestic stocks: 10 percent to 14 percent;
- Foreign stocks: 15 percent to 25 percent; and
- Emerging market stocks: 25 percent to 35 percent.

Figure 2.2   The Impact of Domestic and Foreign Stock Allocations on Standard Deviation

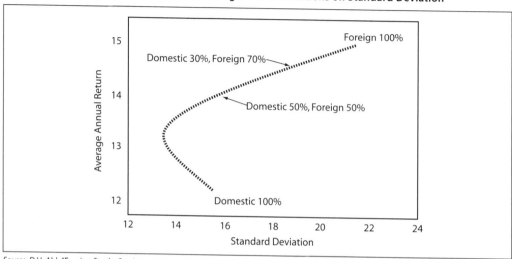

Source: D.H. Ahl, "Foreign Stocks Can Improve Investment Return and Lower Risk," Basic Principles of Investing: A Down to Earth, No-Nonsense Approach. www.swapmeetdave.com/Bible/USForeign.htm (accessed Sept. 25, 2006, checked March 8, 2007).

Table 2.3   Stock Market Returns and Standard Deviation

	Standard Deviation of Returns (%)			
	1 Year	10 Years	25 Years	50 Years
Returns in upper range	25.1%	11.2%	8.7%	7.7%
Returns in lower range	−11.1%	2.4%	4.7%	5.7%
Standard deviation	18.1%	4.4%	2.0%	1.0%

Source: J.M. Bogle, *Common Sense on Mutual Funds*, New York: J. Wiley & Sons (1999). Used with permission.

A demonstration of the value of standard deviation can be seen in Figure 2.2. This illustration compares the risk, as measured by the standard deviation, between domestic and foreign stocks. A portfolio of 100-percent foreign stocks had a much greater risk (standard deviation of 22) with a better return than domestic stocks with a standard deviation of 16. A mix of 50-percent domestic and 50-percent foreign stocks was expected to have a return of 15 percent, but with reduced risk (standard deviation of 14).[4] As a practical matter, most investors in the United States have not been inclined to put 50 percent of their assets in foreign markets.

The risk as measured by the standard deviation continues to decline over time, as shown in Table 2.3.

The standard deviation as used in mutual funds signifies the deviation of the returns from the expected normal returns. Most mutual-fund rating companies, including Morningstar, list the standard deviation of annual returns for the past 5 years or 10 years for rated mutual funds.

Alpha

Alpha is a measure of the excess return added by an investment manager who uses regression analysis to compare his/her returns with a benchmark. It is a good measure of the fund performance vs. a benchmark. If the manager has outperformed the benchmark, the result is a positive number such as 5 percent (an excess return over the benchmark due to the manager's skill in picking the security). A fund manager may take excessive risk, such as the loading up with technology stocks that occurred in the last market surge, in order to generate greater returns. The wise investor may wish to look at 5-year, 10-year, or longer alphas to appreciate the quality of fund managers.

Beta

Beta is a measure of the volatility or risk of a stock in comparison to the overall market. This is also an expression of how much risk an investor wishes to take and helps with the selection of securities based on the risk compared to the market or a sub-sector of the market. A beta of 1 implies that the price fluctuation of that stock moves with the rest of the market (or carries a similar risk as the market). A beta less than 1 means that the stock is less volatile than the market, such as a portfolio of government-issued treasury bills. A beta of more than 1 generally indicates that the stock will fluctuate more than the market; these stocks are typically technology stocks. The problem with beta as a measure of risk alone is that it is too simplistic, gives the investor an idea of past fluctuation only, and does not in any way predict future behavior. In addition, it only measures market risk that cannot be eliminated by diversification, as previously discussed. It does not take into account diversifiable risk or risk specific to the company.

Sharpe Ratio

The *Sharpe ratio* (named after the Nobel Laureate William Sharpe, who devised it) is a more direct measure of risk to reward. This average risk-adjusted return helps an investor or manager find the best possible proportion of securities, including cash, to obtain the best return. Despite the drawbacks of various measures, the Sharpe ratio is a better indicator of performance of a mutual fund than the gross return mentioned in a prospectus.

Table 2.4   Measuring Performance

American Funds Capital World Growth and Income Fund (CWGCX)		
Measure	CWGCX	Category
Alpha (against standard index)	0.43%	–3.61%
Beta (against standard index)	0.84%	0.89%
Mean annual return	20.50%	1.35%
R-squared (against standard index)	94%	79.88%
Standard deviation	8.95%	10.42%
Sharpe ratio	1.82	n/a

Source: www.finance.yahoo.com. Used with permission.

R-Squared

R-squared represents the percent of a fund's movement that can be explained by changes in its benchmark index. The value for R-squared ranges from 0 to 100 with 100 indicating that all the changes in the fund are entirely due to changes in the benchmark index, whereas a 0 signifies the reverse. Ratios greater than 70 are generally considered as being diverse, whereas less than 40 are thought to be more specialized in a sector. It is used in conjunction with alpha or beta values. For example, if a fund has a beta less than 1, but an R-squared value of about 100, it is most likely offering higher risk-adjusted returns. On the other hand, a low R-squared may diminish the significance of a beta.

To put all of these measures in perspective, if the reader looks up American Funds Capital World Growth & Income Fund (CWGCX) on www.finance.yahoo.com, under the "risk" and "three-year" tabs we see the three-year performance of the fund against the overall category in which the funds are grouped. In this case the fund manager has outperformed the benchmark as indicated by a positive alpha, with approximately the same risk (beta), and a significantly better annual return. The R-squared is higher (94 percent) because the particular fund is a diverse portfolio and not concentrated in one particular sector. (See Table 2.4.)

Personal Risk Tolerance

There is no way around eliminating all the market risk. You have to decide which risk you want to take. In addition, you need to plan effectively. If you don't, by the time you pay taxes on your investment earnings, you may have no return because the taxes have eroded your return.

Figure 2.3 What's the Risk vs. Reward of Your Investments?

	Way Above Average (5 points)	Above Average (4 points)	Average (3 points)	Below Average (2 points)	Way Below Average (1 point)	Totals
What is the expected annual return?						
How liquid is the investment?						
Is the investment almost self-managing (you don't have to spend a lot of time on it)?						
Can you get your expected return quickly?						
Does it do well despite inflation?						
Are there tax advantages?						
Is the money you invested safe?						
Is the interest rate fairly steady?						
Does this investment match your personality regarding risk vs. return?						
What is the potential that you'll get the income or return promised?						

TOTAL

Divide TOTAL by 10 ÷10

Final Rating

Adapted by J. Sestina from: J.E. Sestina, *Managing to Be Wealthy: Putting Your Financial Plan and Planner to Work for You,* Chicago, Ill: Dearborn Trade (2000).

Although studying investment performance won't dictate how the stock or fund will perform in the future, it can provide you with an idea of how volatile an investment has been in the past. Two securities can produce the same long-term performance with separate levels of short-term volatility.

When determining your level of risk, you will need to look at the risk within each financial choice you are considering. The risk evaluation checklist in Figure 2.3 can help you compare different investments. It is important that you honestly answer each of the 10 questions. The investment triangle in Figure 2.4 will help you choose investments based on the level of risk that your respective situation allows.

There is clearly a generational divide in risk taking (Table 2.5). Tolerance of the degree of risk is consistent with the fact that younger-age investors are willing to accept above-average risk for substantial gain with the understanding that they will have enough time to recover from an unfavorable outcome.

Figure 2.4   Investment Triangle

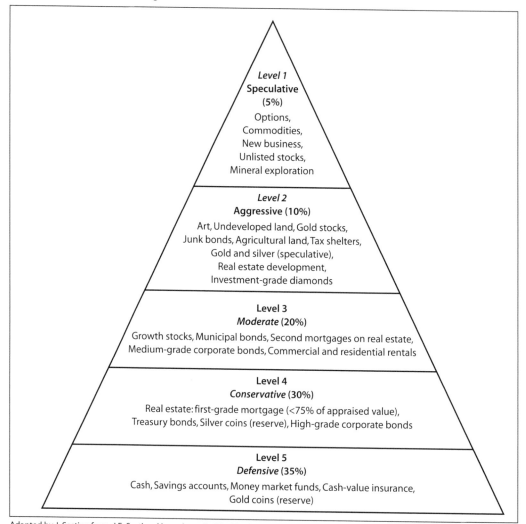

Adapted by J. Sestina from: J.E. Sestina, *Managing to Be Wealthy: Putting Your Financial Plan and Planner to Work for You,* Chicago, Ill: Dearborn Trade (2000).

You only invest as much as your level of risk will allow. If you have X dollars, apply Y percent in the bottom level and work your way up the triangle (Figure 2.4) until you run out of money. With this method, the less money you have to invest, the more conservative you must be. For example, if you only have $10,000 to invest, you might place $3,500 in the defensive level, $3,000 in the conservative level, $2,000 in the moderate level, $1,000 in the aggressive level, and $500 in the speculative

Table 2.5   Investment Risk-Taking by Generation

	Silent (born before 1945)	Baby Boomer (born 1945–1964)	Gen X (born 1965–1975)	Gen Y (born 1977+)
Take substantial risk for substantial gain	5%	5%	9%	11%
Take average or above average risk for average or above average gain	72%	81%	79%	74%
Take no risk or below average risk for lesser gains	23%	14%	12%	15%

Source: S.A. De Vaney, S.T. Chiremba, "Comparing the Retirement Savings of the Baby Boomers and Other Cohorts," *Compensation and Working Conditions Online*, U.S. Department of Labor, Bureau of Labor Statistics. Originally posted: Jan. 24, 2005; Revision posted: March 16, 2005. www.bls.gov/opub/cwc/print/cm20050114ar01p1.htm#14 (Accessed June 29, 2007).

level. Of course, $500 will get you nothing, so you are forced back one level, so you now have $1,500 to put at the moderate level, or back off yet one more level and have $3,500 to invest at the moderate level. Either way, the amount you have to invest forces you to refrain from speculating.

It doesn't matter if you don't agree with the percentages in the investment triangle as long as you understand these three concepts that can help you invest wisely and within your risk tolerance:

- Have an investment plan and stick to it;
- Diversify, but don't spread yourself too thin; and
- Determine the level of risk you can afford.

The investment triangle approach combines these three concepts into a workable method. You will do yourself a favor if you don't make investing more complicated than it is. Always ask yourself, "How does this investment fit my goal?" Invest with a goal in mind. Make sure that your portfolio is structured for meeting your goal and not for performance.

Benchmarks or Market Indices

Market indices are benchmarks for the investor to use to compare his/her return on an investment with the entire stock and bond market, or a specific segment or sector of the market. The most widely used indices for this purpose are:

- **Dow Jones Industrial Average.** This well-known index tracks the stocks of 30 major companies from a mix of industries, including consumer products (Altria Group Inc., and Coca Cola), natural resources (Exxon Mobil), software (Microsoft®), pharmaceuticals (Pfizer Inc.), and others. The list of the 30 companies included in the DJIA changes over time depending upon the strength and stability of the company. Importantly, the index reflects only part of the market; it does not reflect small- or mid-cap stocks or bonds.

- **Standard & Poor's 500 Index (S&P 500).** The S&P 500 is a weighted index of the top 500 companies and is a reflection of large-cap stocks and mutual funds. Certain index mutual funds consist of securities similar to the S&P 500.

- **Dow Jones Wilshire 5000 Composite Index.** The Wilshire index tracks practically all publicly traded companies in the stock market. The index is a capitalization-weighted index and is intended to measure the entire U.S. stock market.

- **NASDAQ Composite Index.** The NASDAQ is an electronic system that consists almost entirely of large technology companies. The index is somewhat volatile compared to the S&P 500 because of the technology companies represented in the index.

- **Russell 3000 Index.** This index consists of 3,000 of the largest U.S. stocks, which represent about 98 percent of the value of the stock market.

- **Russell 2000 Index.** This weighted index tracks 2,000 of the smallest U.S. companies.

- **Lehman Brothers Aggregate Bond Index.** This commonly used benchmark mirrors the U.S bond market including government bonds and corporations.

- **The MSCI EAFE Index.** This is an index of foreign (non-U.S.) stocks and covers equity markets for Europe, Australasia, and Far East. MSCI stands for Morgan Stanley Capital International— Capital is the research arm of American Funds, which is responsible for all of the research behind the index.

Stock Valuations

There are two well-accepted methods of valuing stocks. The relative method compares a stock's valuation with the company's own historic valuation or other stocks. If an investor wished to investigate the value of a pharmaceutical stock such as Pfizer, it would make sense to compare its valuation with other similar-sized pharmaceuticals. The other method is using an absolute or intrinsic value. This value is derived by estimating the present value (see chapter 7, Using Financial Statements to Make Decisions, in Volume 2 of The Smarter Physician Series [©2007 Medical Group Management Association]) of the company's future income stream.

John Bogle, the father of mutual-fund indexing, points to three variables that determine long-term returns in the stock market:[3] the dividend yield at the time of the initial investment; the subsequent rate of growth in earnings of the company; and the change in the price/earnings (P/E) ratio over the period of the investment.

The correct and purest way to value a company is through discounted cash flow. *Discounted cash flow* is what investors are willing to pay today so they can receive anticipated cash flows in the future. Most investors are not financial experts and in lieu of performing complicated discounted cash-flow analyses, they prefer to use simpler rules of thumb. The P/E ratio or "multiple" is the most popular because it is easy to understand. Simply, the P/E ratio equals the price of the stock per share divided by earnings per share.

A P/E ratio tells investors how much they are paying for the company's earning potential. The P/E ratio may either be based on the reported earnings from the latest year (trailing P/E), or the forecast of next year's earnings (forward P/E). As an example, if a stock earned $2 a share the previous year and the current share price is $40, the trailing P/E ratio is 20. If the same stock is forecast to earn $1 per share, the forward P/E is 40. A high P/E for a company (generally found in new and/or fast-growing companies) means investors expect greater earnings growth than in companies with a low P/E (more common to mature companies). Blue-chip companies, in general, tend not to have high P/E ratios. However, they are profitable for investors because they pay regular dividends in contrast to younger companies that may pay a small or no dividend.

P/E ratios are also used to price the stock market as a whole or as a specific index as a measure of how expensive stocks are, compared to historical controls. As an illustration, the average P/E for the S&P 500 was around 15 from 1950 to 2000. Then it jumped to about 30—indicating that stocks were historically overpriced—before the market dipped severely in the year 2000. Relying on the P/E ratio alone is not smart. The ratio is not a substitute for good research.

Some investors prefer the price/earning-to-growth (PEG) ratio, which is the financial ratio of a company. The PEG ratio is the P/E ratio divided by the annual earnings per share growth, which can include historical P/E ratios and growth rates, or estimated future rates. The PEG ratio is a widely used indicator of a stock's potential value. It is favored by many investors over the P/E ratio because it also incorporates growth. A lower PEG (less than 1.0) means that the stock is undervalued in the sense that the market does not expect strong future earnings growth, while a higher ratio (more than 1.0) indicates the opposite, and possibly an overpriced stock. As an example, traditional growth stocks that are stable carry a PEG of around 1.5. In other industries where assets are more important than growth, such as the oil industry or in companies expected to lose money for some time, a PEG ratio is of little help.

Keep in mind that the numbers and ratios used are based on projections, and therefore, can be less than accurate. Also, there are many variations using past earnings for different time periods (for example, one year vs. five years). Be sure to know the exact definition your advisory source is using.

Asset Allocation

Before learning the concept of asset allocation, it is valuable to understand the financial cycle. This is critical because the financial cycle and your tolerance for volatility are related. You likely already know the basics of the financial cycle and don't realize it. For example, what if you could only put your money in money markets or bonds? How would you decide which financial product to choose? What happens when inflation and interest rates rise? Businesses can't afford to finance growth by borrowing money at this time in the cycle. In response, the stock market plummets. This is an ideal time to use money market funds to keep up with rising inflation and interest rates. What happens when interest rates decrease? Businesses and individuals borrow money, and the stock market rises. This is an appropriate time to lock in higher interest rates through medium-term bonds as the rates begin to fall. From year to year, there are many variations of the financial cycle, such as stagflation, disinflation, and so forth. What is most important is that you understand what happens during the basic up-and-down cycles. Regardless of where the financial cycle is on its roller-coaster ride, you should always have a diversified portfolio that contains a mix of stocks, bonds, and cash.

By definition, asset allocation relates to the percentage of money you invest in stocks compared to bonds and other types of assets, such as real estate, commodities, and cash accounts. It is a concept that considers how much you should have in growth and non-growth investments based on past market history. Simply put, asset allocation is all about not putting all of your eggs in one basket. Investment categories—stocks, real estate, bonds, and money market mutual funds—endure ups and downs. Effective asset allocation helps you endure those cycles more easily.

Asset-allocation decisions have been extensively studied. A 1995 study of pension plans by Brinson and colleagues showed that 90 percent of the variability of returns over time can be explained by asset-allocation decisions.[5] Ibbotson and Kaplan in 2000 further studied this subject and demonstrated that the asset-allocation decision explains about 40 percent of the variation of returns across funds and 100 percent of the variation in the aggregate.[6] In his book, *The Intelligent Asset Allocator*, Bernstein (a physician turned money manager) suggests that individual investors ask themselves three questions:[3]

1. How many different asset classes do I want to own? Most people are satisfied with the simplest choices: domestic large stocks, domestic small stocks, foreign stocks, and domestic short-term and long-term bonds. Others may add real-estate investment trusts (REITs), emerging market stocks, foreign small stocks, etc.;

2. How conventional a portfolio do I wish to have? A conventional portfolio may only include domestic large stocks, domestic and foreign small stocks; and

3. How much risk can I tolerate? This means investors choosing the right allocation for them in terms of stocks and bonds. Conservative investors might choose 70 percent bonds and 30 percent stocks, while aggressive investors might choose 25 percent bonds and 75 percent stocks. Most other investors will fall somewhere in between (Table 2.6).

Stocks fluctuate more than bonds, hence the higher-stated risk compared to bonds, although some research would argue that point. This is the reason that most financial advisors advocate a higher percent of stocks in any asset-allocation model early in an investor's career. An allocation ratio of 80:20 or 70:30 (stocks vs. bonds) might be recommended early on; whereas if the time horizon is short, the mix is more conservative, such as 60:40 or 50:50 (stocks vs. bonds) (Table 2.7). This traditional approach has been challenged because a 100-percent bond portfolio is much more volatile (the coefficient of variation is twice as large), and therefore, riskier than a 100-percent stock portfolio. Spitzer and Singh have suggested that a money market portfolio may be less risky and preferable to a bond portfolio in a retirement account.[7]

There is no single asset-allocation strategy that works for everyone or every situation. Your risk tolerance and investment goals will determine how much you put into each investment category. Likely, your ultimate financial goal is to retire and maintain the lifestyle to which you are accustomed.

Table 2.6   Average Annual Total Returns by Asset-Allocation Model

Model	Allocation	Average Annual Total Return, 1976–2005	Years Returns Up/ Total Years	Years Returns Down/Total Years
High-growth investment mix	Growth: 70%; Growth & income: 20%; Bonds: 5%; Cash: 5%	11.1%	22/30	8/30
Moderate-growth investment mix	Growth 45%; Growth & income: 25%; Bonds: 20%; Cash: 10%	10.8%	23/30	7/30
Balanced investment mix	Growth: 25%; Growth & income: 25%; Bonds: 25%; Cash 25%	9.9%	27/30	3/30
Conservative investment mix	Growth: 0%; Growth & income: 30%; Bonds: 40%; Cash: 30%	9.3%	29/30	1/30
Capital preservation investment mix	Growth 0%; Growth & income: 0%; Bonds: 50%; Cash: 50%	7.7%	28/30	2/30

Source: American Funds, 2006. Used with permission.

Table 2.7   50-Year Annualized Returns and Risks for Stocks and Bonds

Mix	50-Year Annualized Returns	Risk (Standard Deviation)
100% stocks	10.4%	16.5%
100% bonds	6.1%	7.6%
40% stocks, 60% bonds	8.1%	9%
50% stocks, 50% bonds	8.6%	9.9%
60% stocks, 40% bonds	9%	11.1%

Source: Stocks: S&P 500 Index. Bonds: S&P High-Grade Bond Index (1954–1973); Lehman Brothers Long-Term High Quality Government/ Corporate Bond Index (1974–1975); Lehman Brothers Aggregate Bond Index (1976–2003).

How soon you retire and in what style you live during retirement will greatly depend on asset-allocation decisions you made years before. That said, it is best to focus on your tolerance for volatility when considering the risks of investing.

Interestingly, one of the most significant investment risks is doing nothing. You cannot embark on your journey to comfortable retirement if you don't take the first step of developing a comprehensive financial plan, which

Figure 2.5   Factors in Successful Investment

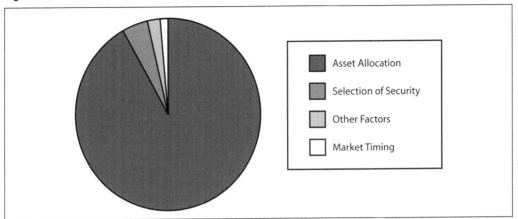

includes an asset-allocation strategy. For decades, computer modeling has been a popular method of determining an investor's asset allocation. There are several software programs that build an asset-allocation plan. Asset allocation is not a one-size-fits-all matter. What is ideal for one investor may not be appropriate for another. For example, a 30-year-old physician who is years away from retirement will have a different strategy than a 55-year-old physician who is nearing retirement and has a limited portfolio. Essentially, successful asset allocation depends on different variables, such as your age, risk profile, family situation, and investment goals. What is not in question is that of all the factors, including the type of stocks and market timing, asset allocation is the most important factor that determines the success or failure of an investment plan (Figure 2.5).

Diversification

Diversification involves investing in the securities of different firms and a variety of industries in an attempt to spread the risk and lessen the likelihood of losses. In the investment game, there are many risks. Even if you never buy a stock or a bond, you must deal with inflation risk. If you place your savings in a savings account that yields 4 percent, and inflation is 3 percent, you're only earning 1 percent on your money, which is your real return. On top of that, you will pay taxes on all taxable gains, dividends, and interest (Table 2.8).

You overcome risk with the investment strategy of diversification. How do you diversify? It doesn't mean buying a little of everything. There are some investments you can't afford. For example, fine art that costs millions of

Table 2.8   Stock and Bond Returns: 1926–1989

	Stock Returns	Bonds
Market returns	534.46%	17.30%
After transaction costs	354.98%	11.47%
After income taxes	161.55%	4.91%
After capital gains	113.40%	4.87%
After inflation	16.10%	0.69%

Source: http://pages.stern.nyu.edu/~adamodar/New_Home_Page/invphillectures/port.html (accessed Sept. 30, 2006). Used with permission.

dollars is likely out of your price range. Some choices don't provide consistent returns, so you don't receive the value of compound interest.

The first step in diversification is deciding how much money you should have in growth investments (such as stocks, real estate, oil and gas, and gold) and how much money you should have in non-growth investments (such as money market mutual funds, bonds, savings accounts, CDs, T-bills, and T-notes).

Next, you need to decide what type of growth and non-growth investments are best for you. Make this decision based on time. How old are you? The longer the time frame you have before you'll need your money, the better you will be able to survive short-term declines in the value of your holdings. Obviously, you expect your portfolio to last until the end of your life. Therefore, if you're 45 years old and you expect to live until age 85, you have a 40-year horizon. Chances are, you won't put a dollar in today and leave it there for 40 years.

With this in mind, we arbitrarily divide the 40-year figure by 2, which gives us a 20-year investment horizon. Over a long-term horizon, stocks have performed better than any other investment. If you are certain that you should be in the stock market, then you should allocate 100 percent of your funds if you can stand the volatility. The main issue, of course, is how to protect against the volatility. This means that you should have enough cash reserves so you don't have to be concerned about the stock market for a long period of time. This reserve should be liquid cash easily accessible 24 hours a day for emergencies. The exact period of time depends on your investment horizon—generally three months for individuals and six months for couples. Remember, don't forget to build a cash reserve, which is liquid cash you can easily access 24 hours a day for emergencies.

Figure 2.6 Stocks vs. Bonds Annual Total Returns

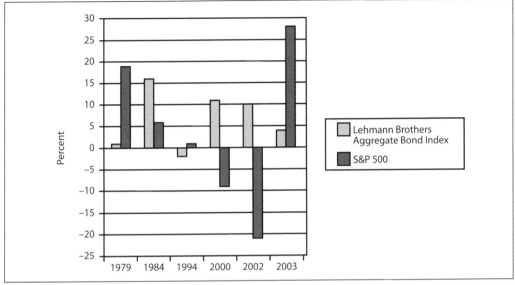

Source: Lehman Brothers, S&P 500.

Non-growth investments protect you from volatility. The strategy becomes evident when annual total returns for the S&P 500 and the Lehmann Brothers aggregate bond index (a surrogate for fixed-income investments) are compared over the past 25 years (Figure 2.6). In the area of non-growth investments, it is the author's preference (Sestina)[8] to buy a bond that matures at a required date. CDs and bank accounts are typically not as successful as other types of non-growth investments. Avoid bond mutual funds when compensating for volatility because bond prices fluctuate.

Laddering can help reduce volatility. It involves buying several bonds so that maturity dates are staggered, rather than pouring all of the investment into one bond. This investment technique will allow you to predict how many dollars will become available to deposit into your money market fund or other liquid investments.

It is easier to see this principle in action during retirement. Take one year of your projected cash flow, add a cost for inflation, and place the amount in a one-year money market fund. Then take the next year's cash flow plus inflation and deposit that into a one-year Treasury bill. Then invest the cash-flow-plus-inflation amounts for years three, four, and five into Treasury bills that have corresponding three-year, four-year, and five-year maturity dates. With this strategy, you have a five-year plan with your investments in a ladder. You have five years to decide when to sell the bonds to provide for year six and onward. Therefore, you don't have to worry about the volatility of the stock market during the five years when your bonds are maturing.

You can use the laddering approach even before retirement. Determine how much non-growth investments you require based on your financial safety needs. Is your job secure? How much money have you saved? How much money do you owe? Developing an emergency fund is recommended. If you don't set aside funds for emergencies, short-term financial issues could require that you dig into your long-term investments at a time that is not ideal, such as in a market downturn. It is helpful to have a portfolio with ample short-term cash and bond investments if you face a financial crisis. Do you want to have one year's worth of income available, or two? Any answer is correct. It depends on you and your specific situation.

When investing, you should prepare your financial plan, know the reasons why you're investing in a particular product to meet your goals, and then take action. Asset allocation is a concept that considers how much you should have in growth and non-growth investments based on past market history.

Also, keep in mind that the odds are against an investor attempting to "time" the stock market. Several studies show that people may get out of the stock market in time, but they don't return to the stock market in time. Buying and selling, and trying to guess highs and lows in the market, has a poor track record as a financial strategy. The average equity investor, not surprisingly, has done poorly over a 20-year period compared to the average equity fund (3.5 percent for the investor vs. 10.2 percent for the index), or compared to the S&P 500. The S&P 500 Index returned almost 13 percent during that same period (Figure 2.7). In addition, efforts at timing may lead to more turnover, and therefore, more cost and tax implications. This is why most investors lose when they attempt to time the market. It is more important to have an effective asset-allocation plan than to time the market. Remember, investments in growth and non-growth areas are essential.

Dividend Reinvestment

Dividend-paying stocks generate exceptional returns for investors in the long term. Long-term investors stick with these stocks because in down or bear markets, they are in a better position. Seigel calls reinvested dividends the "bear market protector" because additional shares of the stock are

Figure 2.7   Growth of $1,000 from 1984–2003

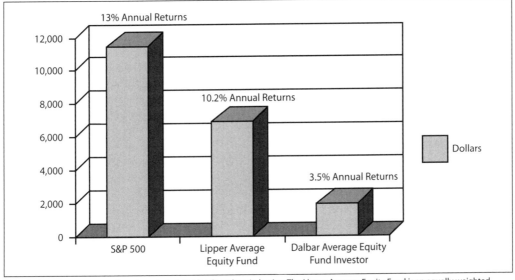

NOTE: Performance assumes reinvestment of all dividends and capital gains. The Lipper Average Equity Fund is an equally weighted average of all equity funds. The Dalbar Equity Fund is the rate of return an equity investor earned based on the amount of time that shareholders actually remained invested in equity mutual funds. The period equals 29.5 months from 1984–2003. Used with permission.

Source: UBS Global Asset Management.

purchased in bear markets. When the market recovers, the same shares are worth more and serve as a "return accelerator."[8,9]

Rebalancing

Once you have selected an asset allocation (stocks, bonds, cash), rebalancing is necessary to make sure the overall allocation is maintained. The movements of the stock and bond markets will change the percentages of the allocations. If small stocks do very well one year, the percentage that small stocks represent in your portfolio will exceed the target you have set. Asset class weightings are typically checked semiannually or annually. They are rebalanced whenever an asset class has changed by more than 5 percent from the target allocation. Many investment professionals suggest setting a date for an annual review and rebalancing, such as the investor's birthday or January 1. Rebalancing takes an enormous amount of discipline. Most investors will find it counterintuitive to sell something that has done well and put money into a sector that has not performed well.

Solving the practical problem of how often to rebalance will depend on whether the account is taxable or non-taxable. For non-taxable accounts, there are no tax consequences to buying and selling in the account; thus, rebalancing annually or even every other year is probably adequate. For taxable accounts, generating capital gains can bring tax liability, so most advisors suggest a yearly rebalancing.

Several options can be used to rebalance a portfolio:

- Adding money from new savings to bring the asset that has decreased up to the target;

- Directing any dividends and capital gains from the overweighted asset classes into those that are underweighted; and

- Transferring or exchanging cash between asset accounts, although the tax implications will need to be assessed.

The goal is to return to the asset-allocation policy you selected or change to one you currently favor.

Remember, the concept of diversification should eliminate the problem that arises when your asset allocation falls out of line with your goals—as it quickly can in a bull market. Armed with knowledge about the financial cycle, risk, and diversifying to reduce risk, two investment choices beyond stocks are obvious: bonds and cash (money market funds and CDs). A third choice recommended for most individuals' investment strategies is mutual funds.

Mutual Funds

For an individual investor, mutual funds are a tremendous way to get started. A mutual fund is a professionally managed corporation that invests in individual investments, such as stocks and bonds. Mutual funds are technically not an asset—at least not the same as stocks, bonds, or cash. Essentially, a mutual fund combines money from thousands of small investors. Then the fund's manager purchases stocks, bonds, or other securities with it.

Advantages of Mutual Funds

The multiple advantages to buying a mutual fund rather than individual stocks are:

- **Professional management.** Instead of spending your time reading and researching the stock market in depth, you benefit from the experience of professional managers and research staff;

- **Affordability and diversification.** You can own more stocks at a lower cost because the fund buys in volume and receives better transaction costs than you could on your own for the amount you have to invest. Mutual funds often allow a lower minimum amount if the investor holds the fund in an individual retirement account (IRA). Thus, you can diversify between different funds even within a small IRA;

- **Liquidity.** Because there is an open market with most funds, they may be bought and sold easily. Usually, you can make changes in your portfolio within a day by making a phone call or via the Internet; and

- **Flexibility.** If you own shares in a fund belonging to a family of funds, you can move back and forth more freely between funds with different styles. In most cases, there is no fee.

Disadvantages of Owning a Mutual Fund

There are disadvantages related to mutual funds, including:

- **Lack of control.** Investors can generally review the approximate distribution of the types of securities within a fund but many details are not available. Nor can they have any influence over the fund's stock selection, purchases, or sales. To most investors, this is an advantage, not a disadvantage;

- **Costs despite negative returns.** Investors must still pay the annual fees, sales charges, and other expenses regardless of whether the fund performs well or not. Capital gains are paid, even though there has not been a sale of the shares from the investor's savings, unlike individual stocks; and

- **Price uncertainty.** Mutual funds usually calculate their net asset value (NAV) at the end of the day after the market closes, so an investor has trouble obtaining the minute-to-minute price of the fund's shares. Again, for the average mutual-fund investor, this is not a disadvantage.

Types of Mutual Funds

There are three types of mutual funds. You can research them in publications by Value Line (www.valueline.com) and Morningstar (www.morningstar.com). Keep in mind that the following are examples, and not recommendations:

Open-end investment companies. You can buy shares from the fund and sell them back to the fund. Vanguard 500 Index and Fidelity Magellan are examples;

Closed-end investment companies. These companies have a fixed number of shares. No new shares are issued. Gabelli Equity and Black Rock Income are examples; and

Investment trusts. You buy an interest in an unmanaged pool of investments. The trust agreement specifies the manner in which the investments are held for safekeeping. There is no trading of these trusts. One type of investment trust is an REIT.

Categories of Funds

There are also multiple categories and sub-categories of mutual funds. Some of the most common are discussed here.

Value funds. Value-fund managers search for stocks they believe are inexpensive on the basis of earnings power, or the value of their underlying assets. Value funds are priced inexpensively in relation to the company's assets, profits, and potential profits. Large-cap value managers typically look for large, battered companies whose shares are selling at discounted prices. Small-cap value managers often search for small companies—usually with a market value of less than $1 billion—that have been shunned by other investors.

Growth funds. For a majority of long-term investors, a growth fund should serve as the core around which the rest of their portfolios are developed. Growth funds include companies experiencing rapidly expanding profits and revenues. Some growth-fund managers purchase shares in companies with above-average revenue and earnings growth. Other growth-fund managers search for the fastest-growing companies before they crash. Consider growth funds if you want high long-term returns and can tolerate the normal ups and downs of the stock market.

Growth-and-income funds. They share a goal with equity-income and balanced funds—to provide steady long-term growth while offering reliable income. Like those funds, there is some combination of dividend-paying stocks and income-producing securities, such as bonds or convertible securities. These funds focus more on growth than equity-income or balanced funds. Therefore, they typically produce the lowest yields.

Balanced funds. These funds strive to maintain 50 percent to 60 percent of holdings in stocks and the rest in interest-paying securities such as bonds and convertibles. This gives them the highest yields.

Equity-income funds. These funds seek similar goals and take similar approaches to growth-and-income and balanced funds, with results generally falling somewhere in the middle.

Specialty and other types of funds. Sector and specialty funds focus on particular sectors, such as technology or health care, instead of diversifying holdings. Keep in mind that the top sector one year may crash the next year. These funds are ideal for investors interested in a specific theme, but prefer to minimize the risk of choosing individual stocks within that sector.

Index funds. Index funds attempt to track market averages, and not beat them, by buying and holding all or a large representative sample of the securities in their target indexes. A majority of managed funds don't beat the market in most years. The concept of an index is to provide average returns to investors. The idea is that if the individual investor earns the average return, and if trading costs are kept below average, the total return for the investor is higher than the average return. Many index funds have beaten actively managed funds (funds managed by professionals that seek to beat the market by actively trading) by keeping the cost of commissions, research, and other expenses very low, leaving a larger portion of the return for the investor. This is the reason their average return before expenses has provided the opportunity for above-average return after expenses.

The performance of the S&P500 as a surrogate of index funds is worth comparing against equity funds in general. From 1967–1997, $10,000 left to grow would yield $216,900 in equity funds (a growth of 10.8 percent) compared to $342,400 in index funds (a return of 12.5 percent).[3] For the same period, index funds have had an advantage of 1.3 percent. The fundamental reason for the difference is the cost advantage of the index funds. Mutual fund costs run about 1.4 percent per year and transaction costs of about 0.5 percent per year for a net cost of 2 percent compared to usual index fund costs of less than 0.5 percent. As far as the risk of both types of mutual funds is concerned, the 10-year standard deviation of the average S&P 500 index fund is 14.30 percent, compared with 14.80 for the average equity fund—a negligible difference.

In addition, most index funds hold their investments longer rather than generate capital gains on repeated trading, and thereby reduce taxes for the investor who keeps index funds in a taxable account. This is why some investors rely on index funds for their taxable accounts, and hold actively managed funds in their tax-deferred or tax-exempt accounts. Not all indexes offer this benefit. Small company indexes change as companies grow. As companies come and go from the indexes, funds that track them must buy and sell to follow suit. A fund's turnover rate is often disclosed in its prospectus or annual reports.

Screening Mutual Funds

To evaluate investments, you can use a grid called an *investment matrix*. The matrix or grid looks like a small checkerboard with labels across the top squares and down one side. Stocks are ranked according to their investment style, and the appropriate box in the grid is shaded. The labels vary among investment-tracking firms. For example, Morningstar uses "large," "medium," and "small" on the vertical side and "value," "blend," and "growth" across the top for a total of nine investment style boxes. Value Line's grid has a rectangle of four boxes with four smaller boxes within each large one. Value Line's labels are "large," and "small" on one side, and "value," and "growth" across the top. Both companies have sample reports on their Websites (www.morningstar.com and www.valueline.com), which demonstrate their investment matrixes.

As you build your portfolio, you may fill all of the categories, large through small. The percentage of your funds placed in each category will depend on where you are in your financial time horizon. You might have six mutual funds that are large-value and three mutual funds that are small-growth.

If you are pursuing a growth strategy, be aware that balanced funds are non-growth investments. They typically contain a large number of bonds that are non-growth investments.

How to Invest in a Mutual Fund

There are many conveniences of investing in mutual funds. A major one is that most fund companies make it easy to invest on a regular basis. Investing regularly is a healthy habit to develop for helping to build wealth, and also for managing the highs and lows of the market. When you invest a fixed amount in a particular fund at regular intervals, the strategy is called *dollar-cost averaging* (DCA). The amount you invest is constant, so you purchase more shares when the price is low, and fewer shares when the price is high. Over time, the average cost of your shares will generally be lower than the average market price per share during that period.

If you participate in an employer-sponsored retirement plan that withholds money from your paycheck, you already benefit from DCA. This is a convenient and systematic option for building an investment portfolio. You can easily budget for the investment amounts because they remain consistent.

DCA does not eliminate the risks of investing in financial markets. Nothing can. DCA also does not guarantee a profit, but it does lower your risk because you are not participating in the market as much as you would by investing immediately. In fact, the median returns for immediate investing are higher than DCA over a long period of time although with greater risk. Be sure to consider your willingness and ability to invest consistently, even during a market downturn. After all, the advantages of DCA depend making regular purchases through the highs and lows.

Income from Mutual Funds

The three ways that investments in a mutual fund can generate income are:

- **Dividend payments.** The fund earns income from dividends and interest paid by the securities owned by the fund. This income is then paid to the shareholders after deducting expenses. Most investors will elect to reinvest the dividends and interest to purchase more shares without paying a sales charge. If the shareholder wants the income, an appropriate number of shares equivalent to the sum are redeemed and the proceeds distributed;

- **Capital gains distributions.** The fund also generates capital gains on the sale of securities within the fund. At the end of the year, capital gains or losses are distributed to shareholders based on the number of shares owned; and

- **Appreciation.** Another source of potential income is when the market value of the fund increases, resulting in appreciation of the shares.

Comparing Returns: Average or Annualized?

Bernstein points out the importance of differentiating between average return and annualized return when trying to evaluate stocks or funds based on performance.[3] As an example, he cites an investor who doubles his investment in a stock (100-percent returns) in the first year and then loses 50 percent in the next year. For example, the share purchase price was $10 per share, it increased to $20 at the end of the first year, and then dropped back to $10 at the end of the second year. The investor basically made no profit from owning the stock, yet the average return was 25 percent. The true picture is given by the annualized return on the stock, which is zero. The average return is a misleading number for investors. It simply reflects the average of each of the annual returns.

Reading the Fund Prospectus

The Securities and Exchange Commission (SEC) requires all mutual funds to include specific categories of information in their prospectuses and to present key data (such as fees and past performance) in a standard format, so that investors can more easily compare different funds. Further information can be obtained by querying the SEC's Electronic Data Gathering Analysis and Retrieval (EDGAR) system database, calling the SEC at 202-551-8090 or faxing at 202-942-9001, or e-mailing to publicinfo@sec.gov.

Before you buy a mutual fund, you should evaluate a fund on three points: objective, return, and cost.

Objectives. You can find the objectives by reading the prospectus. In the first few pages, you will find a description of the fund's objectives. Examples of different objectives are:

- Aggressive growth;
- Growth;
- Growth and income;
- Income;
- Balanced;
- Index;
- International;
- Bond; and
- Money market;

In addition, some funds specialize in certain industrial sectors such as utilities, technology, or health care.

Performance. Perhaps the next most important consideration is performance. The investor needs to know: Who is the fund's manager? How long has that manager been with the fund? What is the track record? Keep in mind that the yield mentioned in the prospectus can be calculated on as little as 5 days' results. There are several mutual-fund tracking reports available that will show the 1-year, 5-year and 10-year performance of various funds. Two of them are offered by Morningstar (www.morningstar.com) and Value Line (www.valueline.com). Also, most business magazines have monthly columns or annual reports on mutual-fund performance. Be sure to conduct ample research before selecting a fund.

Cost. The selling price of the mutual fund is called the *net asset value* (NAV). It is calculated by adding all of the assets owned by the mutual fund and dividing by the number of mutual fund shares that are outstanding. The *buy* price is also called the *public offering price* (POP). This is the cost to the investor to buy one share of a mutual fund. Another key component of a mutual fund's cost to the investor is the amount of fees the mutual fund company or the broker charged the investor to buy, sell, and hold that fund. The following section on fees provides a detailed explanation of the impact these costs can have on the return you actually realize from your mutual-fund investments.

Mutual-Fund Fees

The total costs of any mutual fund may include sales charges, trading costs, and expense ratios. A mutual fund may also levy different fees depending on which type of shares—A, B, or C—of the fund are purchased. No-load funds do not charge a "front-load" fee, but not all no-load funds are low cost. Higher operating expenses may represent a significant and recurring drain on the overall returns, compared with a fund that has an up-front load. You will need to be persistent in discovering these various costs because they are not always mentioned in easily understandable terms in the prospectus.

Sales charge (front-end load). The sales charge on class A shares of a fund is paid by the investor at the time of the purchase of mutual-fund shares. A sizeable portion of the fees goes to the selling agent. The average non-discounted fee for managed funds is between 4 percent and 6 percent. As an example, for a $100,000 investment a 5-percent front-load fee of $5,000 will be paid to the broker or fund company, leaving $95,000 for investment. This fee is discounted for several types of investors, such as those making a large one-time purchase.

Purchase fee. A purchase fee is paid to the fund (not to a broker). It is typically imposed to defray some of the fund's costs associated with the purchase.

Deferred sales charge (back-end load). These charges, which apply to class B shares of a fund, are paid when the shares are sold within a certain of time after purchase. Typically, the full deferred fee is charged for sales made in the first year after purchase, with the fees declining each year to reach zero in the fifth or sixth year. Class B shares may make more sense if held for a long period of time. But the high charges levied on shares in this class have been controversial and the subject of investigation by regulatory authorities.

Class C shares. Purchasing these shares of a fund typically does not involve a front-end sales charge, and deferred charges on sales tend to be lower and of shorter duration than what class B shares may charge. However, class C shares typically impose an annual charge—usually a percentage of the return—for as long they are owned. There may also be 12b-1 fees charged annually. Many advisors recommend that class C shares are more appropriate for a shorter term of ownership.

Exchange fee. A fee is imposed by some funds on shareholders if they exchange (transfer) to another fund within the same fund group or family of funds.

Redemption fee. Another type of fee may be charged by some funds on shareholders when they sell or redeem shares. Unlike a deferred sales load, a redemption fee is paid to the fund (not to a broker).

Trading costs. Trading costs are paid by the fund because they represent a cost of doing business, but they are ultimately passed on to investors, reducing their returns. Trading costs are not part of the expense ratio and can be measured roughly by how often the individual stock portfolio turnover occurs. The smaller the turnover, the more the fund investor benefits. Trading costs are higher for foreign markets, compared to U.S. markets, and for equities compared with bonds.

Expense ratio. This ratio is perhaps the most important one for investors to use when comparing costs between funds. Table 2.9 shows the industry averages for various types of mutual funds.

The expense ratio is required to be disclosed in the prospectus and includes management fees as well as 12b-1 fees, as briefly discussed. Expense ratios can vary from very low (less than 1 percent) to very high (more than 3 percent). Over a long period of time, this ratio will greatly influence total returns.

Table 2.9   Expenses of Mutual Funds by Type

Average Expense Ratio	Percentage
Domestic equities, actively managed	1.55
Domestic equities, passive and index	0.75
International equities, actively managed	1.89
International equities, passive and index	0.95
Fixed income, passive and index	0.39

Management fee. Every fund discloses its management fees in its prospectus. These fees cover everything from salaries to office rent.

12b-1 fee. These fees are often listed separately from management fees and relate to the promotional and marketing expenses of the fund. They are required to be listed in a fund's prospectus. These expenses include advertising and "distribution" fees, or commissions to brokers and financial advisors. This fee can take as much as 1.25 percent of your investment in a fund annually. Most financial advisors recommend avoiding funds with 12b-1 charges.

Exchange Traded Funds (ETFs)

ETFs are immensely popular and their sale has outpaced the growth of traditional index mutual funds. Earlier, ETFs mimicked the S&P 500 and various other stock indices but they now cover most areas including currencies and precious metals. The number of ETFs has exploded to more than 200 with holdings of over $300 billion.[10] The differences between ETFs and index mutual funds are:

1. ETFs have a portfolio made up of an index that reflects a sector (such as health care or commodities) or a market (such as the Pacific) and is not generally selected by a manager. The most well known of all ETFs is the "spider" (SPDR), which stands for Standard & Poor's Depositary Receipts. This ETF copies the 500 largest U.S. stocks and allow an ordinary investor exposure to four-fifths of the market capitalization with the purchase of one share worth $125;

2. ETFs often have lower annual expense ratios compared to index funds. (See Table 2.10.) This is because they are managed passively (not by active money managers) and the expenses do not include the cost of servicing shareholders needs such as bookkeeping, mailing, and other maintenance costs. For example, Vanguard charges an annual expense ratio of 0.19 percent for its Total Stock Market Index and only 0.07 percent for its similar ETF (VIPER);

3. There is a cost for trading ETFs. This is because with a mutual fund the sale goes through the mutual fund company, whereas with an ETF the trade is similar to stock trades and is done through trading market shares. A one-time investment of a large amount from an inheritance, bonus, a settlement, or an IRA rollover is well suited for an ETF;

Table 2.10   ETF Expenses

Fund Type	Basis Points (average expense ratio)
Overall ETFs	40 (0.40)
All equity ETFs	40 (0.40)
Domestic broad market ETFs	19 (0.19)
International equity ETFs	52 (0.52)
Fixed income ETFs	17 (0.17)
Domestic large-cap ETFs	20 (0.20)
Domestic mid-cap ETFs	21 (0.21)
Domestic small-cap ETFs	31 (0.31)

4. ETFs, unlike index mutual funds, are highly liquid and trade throughout the day. One can buy or sell ETFs any time during trading hours, whereas mutual funds are bought and sold at the end of the day;

5. The sale of individual securities within ETFs does not usually result in capital gains, whereas in mutual funds, taxes on capital gains are paid whether or not the shares are sold. The trades within ETFs are not deemed to be taxable because they are exchanges "in kind" (securities in the ETF are traded for mutual fund shares). Certainly, dividends are taxable but taxes on capital gains only result when the shares are sold;

6. ETFs can be useful to construct a customized portfolio of sectors to ensure proper asset allocation and your own investing style. There are allocator models available that can be helpful for guidance in allocating of various ETFs[11]; and

7. ETFs, like mutual funds are also being rated by research firms such as Morningstar and AltaVista Independent Research Inc. The ratings are either based upon comparison to stocks (ratings based on valuation and earnings growth) or mutual funds (ratings based on past performance).[12]

So, which is right for you? It depends on how long you plan to hold the ETF, how much you plan to invest, the difference in annual cost between index mutual funds and the ETF, and whether the sector you are interested in has an index mutual fund available. ETFs are now available for the smallest sector from currencies to nanotechnology. If you invest on a monthly basis in a personal account, the costs of buying an ETF will be a decided disadvantage, despite the lower annual cost. For the same reason, ETFs are not suited for systematic withdrawals such as in a retirement plan, because of the brokerage fees with each transaction. If you have a reasonably large amount to invest at one time, such as a large bonus, and plan to let it grow, the ETF may yield a better return. Most ETFs, particularly in sectors where there is competition from index mutual funds, have annual expenses between 0.12 percent and 0.4 percent. Another supposed disadvantage is that there is not active management of the fund. That may be an advantage, however, as most active fund managers have failed to match index fund results such as the S&P 500.

Overall Investment Strategy

When you invest, you need to measure and define your return so you can monitor the progress. Here are five measures of how your investment is doing:

- What is the cash flow? Is income needed? If so, what range is acceptable?

- Is your investment appreciating? What balance do you want between income and appreciation?

- Are you building any equity?

- Is the investment advantageous for your tax situation?

- Consider the interaction between investments. Can one investment offset the taxable gains of another?

Nobody is perfect, especially in investing. Some common investment mistakes are discussed below.

Not planning. You must have a financial plan to meet your financial goals. Remember that successful investing isn't measured by how many stocks you buy or sell, or what percent return you make. You are successful when you meet your goals.

Over-commitment. Don't commit all of your excess funds. If you consistently have a surplus of, say, $3,000 in your savings or checking account every month, go ahead and invest it. Be sure, though, that you're not investing your cash reserve.

Avarice. Do you try to wring the last penny out of a winning investment? Don't be tight-fisted and hold onto an investment for fear that you'll lose a dime, even when you've already made a dollar. Many financial advisors recommend a half-at-double strategy: Once you've doubled your money, sell half of the investment.

Financial gluttony. Financial gluttons have eyes bigger than their purses. Gluttons become so impatient that they trade too much. They think they will generate a higher return, but all they generate is more commission for the broker. To prevent financial gluttony, remember the magic of compounding, which is demonstrated by the Rule of 72. Use it to estimate how many years it will take to double an investment by dividing the investment's rate of return into 72. For example, an investment that pays a 5-percent return will double in 14.5 years; a 7-percent return will take 10.2 years to double; and a 10-percent return takes about 7.2 years to double. Don't be distracted by the hope of making more. Have the discipline to create a plan and stick to it.

Gullibility. Don't believe everything you hear about an investment and buy on a hunch, tip, or rumor. Buy based on the facts. Consider any "hot tip" you hear just a rumor. Remember that insider trading is illegal, not just for the insider who gives out the tip, but for the purchaser as well.

Sloth. Investing requires hard work. Some people spend more time buying a car than they do learning about the investment they're considering. Do your homework. Find out everything you can before signing your name and dropping your money. Once you make an investment, supervise it. Don't turn over your financial affairs and investments to someone else. At the very least, keep in touch so you know what is happening, and your advisor knows you are a concerned investor. Nobody cares more about your money than you.

Pride. Don't let pride interfere with your financial plan. When you make a mistake, admit it and move on. Stubborn pride makes you ride a loser all the way down. When your investment no longer fits your plan, drop the investment.

Cowardice. Sometimes it is fear of failure—not pride—that trips you up. There is risk in financial planning. Driving a car is risky, but with defensive-driving techniques, you can minimize the risk. You need a financial plan. If you do nothing, you face the risk that inflation will eat away at your purchasing power. Someone else will make the wrong decisions for you about your money, and changes in tax laws will take even more from your pocket.

Conformity. Don't follow the herd. When an investment is recommended in the media, wait a week or two until the price settles down. The institutions buy before the little guy, and then the institutions sell after the little guy buys, and you lose. Buy an investment only if it fits your plan, not because everyone else is doing it.

Over-diversification. It is important to diversify your investments. If one part of your portfolio experiences a loss, you have a better chance that the other parts will not. Still, don't spread yourself too thin. As a general rule, the risk of a portfolio will decrease as the number of stocks in the portfolio increases up to a certain point. With just 7 to 10 stocks, the standard deviation is in the low 20s. Increasing the number of stocks owned brings only a gradual decline in risk. Even with 40 or more stocks, there remains the market risk associated with investing in the market, which is about a 20-percent standard deviation. This means there's a 1-in-5 chance that any one stock will make more or less money than the rest of the market.

Under-diversification. There is no investment for all seasons. It would be easy if you could park your money in one investment and return 30 years later to take your profits. Unfortunately, there are a few financial advisors who believe this, and want you to believe their advice. It is not true. The financial cycle causes fluctuations in the value of all investments at one time or another.

Speculation. Ego is an obstacle in investing. We all want to hit a financial home run. You can't afford the risk. Some advisors will speculate when a client is young, but it is tremendously risky. Why speculate when you can meet your goals without it? Don't postpone your financial freedom even for one year.

Bargain hunting. Don't buy because the investment looks like a bargain. There are no bargains. Buy quality.

Following fads. Don't buy fad investments either. There will always be fads. Usually, they don't last long enough to be worth your time or money. Buy known financial products that will be here today and tomorrow.

Listening to so-called experts. Don't assume that an expert in X is an expert in Y. When you find experts in widgets, it is human nature to ask their opinion on thingamajigs. However, just because they have an opinion doesn't mean they know what they're talking about.

For some investors, the stock market is the only place to be. They enjoy the excitement of investing in a stock to become part-owners of that corporation and having a stake in the company's future financial performance, good or bad. The risks of individual stock purchases are many. Yes, thriving companies sometimes pay out part of their profits by distributing dividends. Others reinvest those profits to bolster future sales, which may increase the value of your shares. The problem with buying individual stocks is that unless you have at least $100,000 to invest, transaction costs, combined with capital gains taxes, can eliminate most or all of your profits. That's assuming you make any profits. Worse, with less than $100,000 to invest you won't be able to diversify your investments to spread the risk among several companies in several industrial sectors.

Finally, there are the factors of information and time. Can you get access to unbiased, in-depth research about individual companies? Do you have time to manage all that information in order to guide your portfolio? For many, the answer is "no" to both questions. Even with the power of the Internet and financial analysis software, it will take many hours a week to adequately monitor a portfolio of individual stocks. Remember, even the experts who do this for a living lose money some of the time. For these reasons, many physicians and other investors choose to learn how investments work (which you have started by reading this chapter), but consult with experts to help them manage their investments.

References

1. AXA Financial Advisors LLC, "Long-term Investing: Remember Inflation," www.axaonline.com/rs/3p/sp/5015.html (accessed Sept. 28, 2006).

2. J.M. Bogle, *Common Sense on Mutual Funds*. New York: J. Wiley & Sons (1999).

3. W. J. Bernstein, *The Intelligent Asset Allocator*. New York: McGraw Hill (2001).

4. D. Ahl, "Foreign Stocks Can Improve Investment Return and Lower Risk," www.swapmeetdave.com/Bible/USForeign.htm (accessed Sept. 25, 2006).

5. G.P. Brinson, B.D. Singer, and G.L. Beebower, "Determinants of Portfolio Performance II: An Update," *Financial Analysts J*, 51 (1) (1995): 133–138.

6. R.G. Ibbotson and P.D. Kaplan, "Does Asset Allocation Policy Explain 40, 90, or 100 Percent of Performance?" *Financial Analysts J*, 56 (1) (2000): 26–33.

7. J.J. Spitzer and S. Singh, "Asset Allocation in the Presence of Varying Returns, Contribution Scenarios and Investment Horizons," *J Financial Planning*, www.fpanet.org/journal/articles/2003_Issues (accessed July 25, 2006).

8. www.sestina.com.

9. J.J. Seigel, *The Future for Investors*, New York: Crown Business (2005).

10. W. Updegrave, *Money*, May (2006): 121–123.

11. www.ishares.com (accessed May 21, 2006).

12. E. Laise, "How to Rate the ETF Ratings" *Wall Street J*, April 29 (2006): B4.

Chapter 3

Investing in Bonds and Other Fixed-Income Instruments

At a basic level a bond is a contract between a lender (investor) and a company or municipality that promises to repay a loan with interest. The borrower needs the money to finance public projects or factories, and issues bonds to borrow capital from the public. Bonds are called *fixed-income investments* in the sense that the issuer of the bond promises to pay the lender a fixed amount at some future date. This is in contrast to dividends from stocks where the company is not bound to pay the stockholder. Bonds do not have as jazzy an image as stocks; however, most advisors recommend their clients add bonds as part of a diversified portfolio. Bonds are generally regarded as less volatile than stocks, but have inherent risks associated with them. Inflation, for example, represents a big risk because it decreases the future value of today's dollar.

Inflation is a decline in the purchasing power of a dollar (in the United States) over time due to the increasing cost of goods and services. A dollar today is worth much more now than it will be years into the future because the dollar loses value over time. As an example, if an investor purchased a certificate of deposit (CD) of $10,000 at 5 percent interest for 12 months, the person expects to receive the principal plus $500 in interest for a total of $10,500 at the end of a year. If inflation is 10 percent and the same investor had purchased $1 of one ounce of gold at the same time, it would cost $1.10 to buy the same ounce of gold at the end of the year. Therefore, the same $10,000 that would have netted 10,000 ounces of gold at the beginning of the year can only acquire 9,550 ounces of gold (which is $10,500 divided by $1.10). In short, the interest payment of 5 percent on the CD would not make up for the loss of purchasing power of 10 percent. It is important to adjust for inflation when one looks at capital-budgeting decisions. In the example cited, the investor in retrospect may have been smarter to buy the gold rather than the CD (not that buying gold is being recommended by the author).

To account for inflation, a consistent apples-to-apples comparison is necessary by applying either a real interest rate or a nominal (or stated) interest rate when forecasting future cash flows. When economists speak of *real dollars*, they mean dollars adjusted for inflation or purchasing power, whereas a *nominal dollar* is the actual cash flow observed. Lenders realize the inflation risk and build in a premium for the expected future (not past) risk of inflation.

Another risk built into the price of bonds is the risk of default. Because the risk of default for government-issued U.S. Treasury bonds is almost zero, the investments have a lower interest rate. Low-rated bonds ("junk bonds") carry a greater risk of default, and therefore, the borrower pays a higher interest rate to the purchaser of the bond. The difference between the interest rate on a Treasury bond and a corporate bond is called a *default risk premium*.

The third important risk in bonds, especially short-term bonds is the reinvestment risk. As an example, if investors purchase long-term bonds and interest rates then rise, the price of these bonds drops. In contrast, if investors purchase short-term bonds, and interest rates are lower at the time the bond matures, they are forced to reinvest the proceeds from the bond into a lower interest-paying bond. Because interest rates are not predictable and the risks of owning short- or long-term bonds are different, most investors use various techniques to diversify their bond holdings.

Bond Terms

When dealing with bonds, it is important to understand the terminology, explained below.[1,2,3,4]

Price. Bonds are priced at par, discount, or at a premium.

Par value. This is the face value of the bond or the dollar amount assigned to the bond when it is first issued by an entity. In general, par value is $1,000 for corporate bonds, but may be higher (often $10,000) for government or some corporate bonds. Municipal bonds are generally bought and sold in minimum lots of 5 bonds (or $5,000 at $1,000 per bond).

Current yield. This is the annual interest rate paid by a bond, as a percentage of its current market price. The primary determinant of pricing bonds is "yield to worst"—either yield to maturity or yield to call in the case of a premium bond. This is different from *required yield*, which is the yield a bond must offer in order for it to be competitive with similar bonds in the market with similar maturity and credit risk.

To find current yield, divide the annual dollar interest rate paid by market price and multiply the result by 100 percent. For example, if a bond that cost $1,000 pays $100 a year in interest, then its current yield is $100 divided by $1,000; multiply the result by 100 to get 10 percent. The current-yield calculation tells investors how much cash income they may receive in a particular year, but it does not take into account any potential gain or loss on the investment.

Coupon rate. The amount of interest the bondholder receives, expressed as a percentage of the par value, is the coupon rate. As an example, if a bond has a par value of $1,000 and a coupon rate of 5 percent, the purchaser of the bond will receive $50 a year. The issuer of the bond will also specify how often the interest will be paid. Typically, most bonds pay interest semi-annually.

Maturity date. The date when the purchaser receives the principal back from the bond issuer, at which time all interest payments cease, is the maturity date. If the bond is a callable bond, the issuing company may, if circumstances demand and if so specified upon issue, decide to return the principal back to the purchaser (or lender) sooner than the maturity.

Yield-to-maturity (YTM). Yield-to-maturity is an accurate indicator of the total return (present value of all future cash flows) an investor may expect by holding the bond until maturity.

Most often, the market rate at which the bond is purchased is different from the par value of the bond. The investor then needs to know:

- the coupon rate (the annual payment made by the bond issuer as a percent of the par value);

- the current yield (as explained before); and

- the YTM (as mentioned, the sum of all the payouts, coupons, and any capital gains or losses).

Suppose you purchased a corporate bond for $950 (at a "discount" as described in the "Premium" section) with a par value of $1,000, a coupon rate of 7 percent, and a maturity date of 4 years.[5] As defined, the coupon payment will be 7 percent of par value ($1,000) for a total of $70. The current yield is 7.37 percent ($70 ÷ $950) and the YTM is 8.53 percent. The multistep calculation to find the YTM amount can be made simpler by using online calculators, such as those found at www.investinginbonds.com or www.motleyfool.com. An easy way to remember these terms is to keep in mind that the coupon rate is the lowest value followed by the current yield and then the YTM, which is the higher number. [5]

Premium. If the price of the bond at a particular time is greater than the par value at which it was issued, then it is said to be priced at a *premium.* This happens when the interest rate on an older bond is higher than current interest rates. If the price is less than the par value, the bond is said to be selling at a *discount.* This occurs when the interest rate on the older bond is lower than the current market rate for bonds of similar maturities or when the ability of the borrower to repay the loan has diminished.

Assessing Bond Investments

Applying the knowledge from chapter 7, Using Financial Statements to Make Decisions, of Volume 2 of The Smarter Physician Series (©2007 Medical Group Management Association) regarding the time value of money, the price of the bond is the sum of all the coupon (interest) payments expected, plus the present value of the bond's par value at maturity.

An investor counts on receiving the principal back at the maturity date of the bond. In the meantime, bond prices will vary and will be trading above or below the par value depending on the prevailing interest rate for bonds of similar maturity and quality. If the investor decides to sell the bond prior to maturity, he/she will have to sell it at the going price. As an example, you purchased ten $1,000 bonds ($10,000) from GoodHealth Corporation in 1980 at a coupon rate of 5 percent with a maturity date of Dec. 31, 2010 and annual interest payments of $500 a year. Let us assume you decide to sell the bonds on Dec. 31, 2000, a time when intermediate interest rates have declined to 2.5 percent. If others bought your bonds, they would still receive $500 a year (5 percent) in interest compared to the 2.5 percent current bonds are paying. Therefore, your bonds may be an attractive buy compared to the current coupon rate, and they would sell for a premium or above par value. Similarly, if the interest rates increased to 10 percent, newly issued bonds might be more attractive than your 5-percent bond, possibly making it less attractive as a result of it selling for a discount or below par value.

After understanding the relationship between interest rates and price, one would assume that for a current bond holder a decrease in interest rates is the best scenario. However, if higher coupon bonds are called, the investor who is relying on the income from the bonds now has to replace older bonds with newer, lower-yielding bonds, which is known as *reinvestment risk.*

Another important variable is the maturity of the bond. The market risk from interest rates is greater with bonds of long maturities than those of shorter maturities. Prices of long-term bonds are more sensitive to changes in interest rates. Therefore, the coupon returns, in general, for long-term bonds are higher to compensate the investor for the additional market risk. However, there are times when the short-term yields exceed long-term rates (inverted yield curve). This is the reason some investors resort to "laddering" bonds. Bonds with staggered maturities are bought with the idea that short-term bonds with smaller yields and low volatility are mixed with long-term bonds with higher yields and greater sensitivity to interest rate fluctuations, and therefore, greater risk. Some investors utilize a "barbell" strategy with short-term and long-term bonds laddered to diversify the risk.

In summary, things to check before buying a bond are:

- **The credit quality.** Credit-rating agencies such as Fitch's and Moody's issue ratings of municipal bond credit strength;

- **The call provision.** A call provision gives the issuer corporation or entity the right to redeem the bonds held by an investor. One reason would be a significant decline in interest rates that will allow the issuer to reissue new bonds with lower coupon rates, thus saving the issuer interest expense; and

- **The bond insurance.** Certain lower-rated or non-rated issuers will acquire insurance from specialty insurance companies that will guarantee timely payment of interest and principal. This insurance generally raises the cost of issuance. At the same time, it provides a lower- or non-rated issuer the opportunity to issue bonds with as much as a AAA rating, thus lowering overall interest costs.

Municipal Bonds

Municipal bonds are obligations issued by cities, towns, counties, states, local public housing authorities, water districts, school districts, and other governmental or quasi-governmental entities.[6,7] These bonds can pay interest dividends that are tax free. The two major categories of municipal bonds are:

- **General obligation bonds.** These bonds are, in essence, guaranteed based on the full faith and credit of the government entity that issues them. This means the government entity is allowed to raise taxes to assure that the bond principal and interest are paid as agreed; and

- **Revenue bonds.** These are issued by entities to finance a specific project, such as an airport, sports stadium, water and sewer development, hospitals, and mass transit systems. The project revenue is then used to pay the principal and interest.

Individual Bonds

Individual bonds can be purchased with a minimum face value of $5,000. Generally, an investor should purchase more than one issue to provide adequate portfolio diversification. The after-market for municipal bonds is not as extensive as other bond markets. This sometimes makes it difficult to sell at a reasonably competitive price before maturity.

Bond Unit Trust or Unit Investment Trusts

Bond unit trust or unit investment trusts allow purchasers to earn a constant yield on purchased bonds because the trust sells the interest in a fixed portfolio of municipal bonds. However, because they sell on the open market like mutual funds or stocks, the value of the trust will vary depending on the market. The trust is created for the secondary market by brokerages. It is designed to expire when the last bond matures, although generally a trust is open for many years.

Portfolios of Bonds

It is possible to purchase municipal bonds through mutual funds that specialize in these investments, which then produce tax-free earnings. A diversified mutual bond fund also may include municipal bonds as a component of its portfolio.

Corporate Bonds

Corporations incur debt for their financial needs by selling stock as well as by going to the public securities markets to sell bonds. To make their bonds more attractive than government bonds, they must sell the bonds at a higher interest rate to attract buyers because corporate bonds obviously carry more risk of default. The interest rate they can offer depends on several factors, one of which is the corporation's credit rating. If the company's credit rating is below investment grade, the bonds issued are called *junk bonds* or *high-yield bonds*. Some corporate bonds are called *convertible bonds* because they can be converted into common stock of the issuer.

Zero-Coupon Bonds

Most of the *zero-coupon bonds* (also called "*zeros* or *ZCBs*")[8,9] are offered by the U.S government, corporations, or state and local governments. The acronym-based names of these bonds include TIGRS and CATS. To understand the concept of zero-coupon bonds, it is important to remember how conventional bonds work. With conventional bonds, investors purchase the bond by paying the face amount of the bond; then they receive interest payments every six months based on the coupon, or interest rate, offered when the bond is sold. At maturity, investors then are reimbursed the full principal amount invested (the exact face amount). With a zero-coupon bond, the bond is sold at a discount from its face value. As previously mentioned, a discount is anything selling below its par value.

The purchaser of a zero-coupon bond receives no interest payments (phantom interest) for the life of the bond. When the bond matures, the bond holder receives the full face amount. It is equal to the initial investment plus the accumulated interest rate compounded over the time the investor held the bond. For example, a purchaser could buy a 20-year municipal zero-coupon bond with a face amount of $32,000 for an initial payment of approximately $10,000. At maturity, the purchaser receives not only the $10,000, but also interest payments ($32,000 − $10,000 = $22,000) calculated at 6 percent compounded annually. When the bond matures, the investor receives the full face amount or $32,000.

The primary advantage of purchasing a zero-coupon bond is that investors are purchasing the bond at a discount, and all future interest payments compound at the original purchase rate. This eliminates all reinvestment risk for that issue or your entire portfolio of zero-coupon bonds. Although most zero-coupon bonds are purchased through a broker, investors can also buy them in denominations of $1,000 and discounted from the face value of 50 percent to 75 percent, depending on the maturity period, through a mutual fund.

Common Types of Zero-Coupon Bonds

There are several types of zero-coupon bonds.

U.S. Treasury Bonds. Separate trading of registered interest and principal securities, or STRIPS are Treasury bonds issued by the U.S. government. They are non-callable, and generally considered the safest bond because they are backed by the full faith and credit of the U.S. government. The term *stripping* refers to the fact that the zero-coupon bond is deposited with a trustee, and the trustee separates the bond into its individual payment components. This allows the components to be registered and traded as individual securities. The actual interest payments are called *coupons*, so named because of their source of cash flow. The residual is what is left of the zero-coupon bond after the interest coupons are stripped. Therefore, a zero-coupon bond consists of both the coupons and the residual.

Municipal zero-coupon bonds. Because these bonds offer tax-free interest, on a taxable-equivalent basis, they may generate a higher return than other bonds. The Bond Market Association notes that "Municipal zeros generally also offer a high degree of safety because the interest earned is usually tax free, and can generate higher returns when calculated on a taxable-equivalent basis."[4] A purchaser of a state-issued zero-coupon bond may also receive the interest free of state income tax.

Advantages of zero-coupon bonds. Zero-coupon bonds are issued in varying maturities from 1 to 40 years. They can be purchased to coincide with a specific long-term financial goal such as retirement or college tuition for children.

Disadvantage of zero-coupon bonds. Tax must be paid on a taxable zero-coupon bonds, even though the interest income has not been received by the purchaser. In other words, there is no cash flow, but taxes must be paid on the "phantom" interest. It may make sense to purchase taxable zero-coupon bonds in a tax-sheltered retirement account, such as a 401(k) plan, IRA, or similar account. Zero-coupon bond prices may also fluctuate more than regular bonds because the payoff for the bond is not until it matures, at which time the bond holder receives the combined principal and accrued interest.

Agency Bonds

These are bonds issued by quasi-governmental agencies. One consideration to note is that safety from default is not guaranteed by the full faith of the issuing agency. The bonds, therefore, must offer better yields for the higher risk taken by the investor. There is usually some collateral such as real-estate mortgages or loans upon which the bonds are issued. Examples of these bonds are: the Government National Mortgage Association (GNMA, or "Ginnie Mae"), Federal National Mortgage Association (FNMA, or "Fannie Mae"), Federal Home Mortgage Corporation (FHMC, or "Freddie Mac"), and the Student Loan Marketing Association (SLMA, or "Sallie Mae").

Stocks or Bonds? The statement that the yield on a Treasury note or bond moves in the opposite direction to its price is heard repeatedly. It is important to understand this aspect of bond mechanics if an investor is to make decisions on buying bonds. When yield goes up, Treasuries and bonds become more attractive to the individuals and institutions (compared with stocks) that have fixed asset-allocation ratios in their portfolios. However, as yields rise or fall, some investors have to calculate the point at which Treasuries/bonds are relatively more expensive than stocks. Some investors use a rule that says: If the earnings yield on the S&P 500 (calculated as projected earnings for the next year divided by current price of the stock, which is the exact reverse of the price/earnings ratio) is lower than the yield on the bond/Treasury, the stock is cheaper than the bond. Assuming a 10-year Treasury bond yields 5.05 percent compared to estimated earnings yield for the S&P 500 of 6.85 percent, the stocks, in general, are more attractive.

Taxable vs. Tax-Free Bonds

To manually compare the equivalent yield on a tax-exempt bond to a taxable investment or vice versa, two pieces of information are needed to calculate the third as follows:

1. Yield on the tax-free bond = 3 percent;

2. Marginal tax rate = 0.39 percent; therefore

3. Equivalent taxable investment to be comparable to tax-free yield = 3 ÷ 1 − 0.39 = 2.61 percent.

Similarly, to calculate the tax-free yield necessary to match a known taxable investment return:

1. Taxable investment return = 3.7 percent;

2. Marginal tax rate = 0.39 percent; therefore

3. Equivalent tax-free yield to be comparable = (3.7) × (1 − 0.39) = 2.257 percent.

Another way to decide whether to invest in taxable or non-taxable bonds is to use an online calculator such as that found on www.investinginbonds. com which can take into account both the federal and your state's income rates when calculating taxable-bond returns.

Diversification offers protection over the long term from the uncertainty that is an indisputable part of investing in the market. The long-term investor, based on past performance, can reasonably conclude that stocks will, in general, generate 3 percent to 4 percent returns from appreciation and another 3 percent to 4 percent from dividends. Therefore, if one deducts a 3-percent inflation adjustment,[10] the real return (adjusted for inflation) on stocks is estimated to be between 3 percent and 5 percent annually. In general, unless an investor is in a low tax bracket, non-taxable bonds outside a retirement portfolio are recommended by most experts. Another decision on whether to buy short-term or long-term bonds also depends on what happens to interest rates, since bond prices fall when interest rates rise and vice versa.

Bond Funds

Bond funds may offer the investor another choice depending on the amount of cash available, the liquidity desired, and the need for diversification. Bond funds, similar to stock funds, are designed for specific objectives such as current income, current tax-exempt income, total return, or to mimic the performance of a market index. The fund may invest in a particular type of bond (government, municipal, mortgage, or high-yield), or varying maturity ranges from short-term (3 years or less), intermediate-term (3 to 10 years), or long-term (10 years or longer).

Bond funds usually make monthly or quarterly dividend payments, not the semi-annual payments made by individual bonds. Similar to stock funds, bond fund prices are based on net asset value (NAV), or the total market value of the portfolio divided by the total number of fund shares outstanding. The NAV generally changes with daily market conditions and activity within the fund. Bond mutual funds can be actively managed or indexed, open-end, closed-end, or exchange-traded funds. In general, individual bonds (not Treasuries) are better suited for investors with at least $100,000 to invest so they can diversify the risk of owning a few bonds. Bond funds are relatively cheap through discount sellers, offer diversification, and offer either monthly income or regular reinvestment options.

Summary

Fixed-income investments such as CDs and bonds are part of an overall strategy for getting an investor to the finish line. Because very few "experts" really know if the market is going to go up or down, or whether inflation will increase or decrease, the best plan is to hedge against all the possible downside risks as much as possible. Laddering allows investors to diversify by investing in bonds of short- and medium-term duration. Therefore, this allows picking up the yield, but not the risk of long-term bonds. When buying bond funds, cost is an important consideration. For most physicians who are in a high-income tax bracket (more than 35-percent tax bracket), a portfolio of municipal bonds is worth considering.

References

1. The Bond Market Association, "Putting Compound Interest to Work with Zero Coupon Bonds," Investing in Bonds.com, www.investinginbonds.com/learnmore.asp?catid=6&id=46 (accessed Sept. 25, 2006).

2. The Motley Fool, "What is a Bond?" www.fool.com/school/basics/investingbasics005.htm (accessed Sept. 25, 2006).

3. Wikipedia, "Bond," http://en.wikipedia.org/wiki/Bond (accessed Sept. 25, 2006).

4. The Bond Market Association, "Markets in Depth," Investing in Bonds.com, www.investinginbonds.com (accessed Sept. 25, 2006).

5. MoneyChimp.com, "Bond Yield-to-Maturity," www.moneychimp. com/articles/finworks/fmbondytm.htm (accessed Dec. 11, 2006).

6. The Bond Market Association, "An Investor's Guide to Municipal Bonds," Investing in Bonds.com, www.investinginbonds.com/info/ igmunis/an_investors_guide_to_municipal_bonds.pdf (accessed Sept. 25, 2006).

7. U.S. Securities and Exchange Commission, "Bonds, Municipal," SEC.gov, modified Feb. 23, 2005, www.sec.gov/answers/bondmun.htm (accessed Sept. 25, 2006).

8. U.S. Securities and Exchange Commission, "Zero-Coupon Bonds," SEC.gov, modified Feb. 1, 2001, www.sec.gov/answers/zero.htm (accessed Sept. 25, 2006).

9. Investopedia.com, "Zero-Coupon Bond," www.investopedia.com/ terms/z/zero-couponbond.asp (accessed Sept. 25, 2006).

10. B. Graham and J. Zweig, *The Intelligent Investor*, rev. ed., New York: Harperbusiness Essentials (2003).

Additional Resources

Federal Home Mortgage Corporation (FHMC, or "Freddie Mac")— www.freddiemac.com

Federal National Mortgage Association (FNMA, or "Fannie Mae")— www.fanniemae.com

Fitch Inc.—www.fitchratings.com

Government National Mortgage Association (GNMA, or "Ginnie Mae")—www.ginniemae.gov

Moody's Investor Service, Inc.—www.moodys.com

Student Loan Marketing Association (SLMA, or "Sallie Mae")— www.salliemae.com

Chapter 4

Do Your Assets Correlate?

Asset correlation is commonly mentioned in investment discussions. But it is seldom explained in detail—even though it is critical for any diversification strategy.

Allocating to different assets (such as stocks and bonds, which move up and down under different market conditions) helps you offset one asset's falling returns with another's rising ones. This strategy helps you lower portfolio risk as you protect against big losses, putting you in a position to achieve better overall portfolio performance—the basic idea behind asset correlation.

How Asset Correlation Works

Statistically, correlation captures the linear relationship between two variables. In portfolio management theory, it shows whether, and how strongly, selected assets are related. "Correlation measures the strength of the historical relationship between two securities' returns," says Leonard Govia, participant advice manager, TIAA-CREF. "It measures how much the returns of any two or more securities are related, but does not imply that the movement of one security causes the movement of another, or that this relationship will exist in the future." (*Securities* is another word for investments.) Correlation ranges from +1.0 to –1.0, where +1.0 equals perfect positive correlation, –1.0 equals perfect negative correlation, and 0.0 equals zero correlation.

To see how asset correlation works, we'll consider a few examples describing how four hypothetical mutual funds perform alone and in combination over an imaginary six-year period. We'll examine three tables in which the funds' risk is represented by their hypothetical *standard deviation*, the measure of a security's volatility (the tendency of a security to rise or fall sharply in price). To simplify the discussion, we'll examine two funds at a time. When the funds are combined in a portfolio, it will consist of a 50-percent allocation to each fund.

Positive Correlation

Assets with a perfect positive correlation have a perfect linear relationship, which means by knowing how the return of one security behaves (rises or falls), you will be better able to forecast what the other security will do.

Table 4.1   Positively Correlated Funds

Year	Fund A	Fund B	Portfolio AB
1	32%	32%	32%
2	−11%	−11%	−11%
3	−14%	−14%	−14%
4	33%	33%	33%
5	−8%	−8%	−8%
6	28%	28%	28%
Average return	10%	10%	10%
Standard deviation	23%	23%	23%

Reprinted with permission from TIAA-CREF's *Advance* magazine, June 2006 issue.

For example, if security A's return goes up, you can expect security B's return to rise as well; you just can't know by how much.

In Table 4.1, hypothetical mutual funds A and B have identical returns over a six-year period and have perfect positive correlation. When fund A's return goes up, fund B's also goes up. When fund A's return drops, so does B's.

Table 4.1 also illustrates that the hypothetical portfolio combination of funds A and B has exactly the same overall return as does either fund by itself. The risk of this portfolio, as measured by the standard deviation, is identical to the standard deviation of either fund alone, so there's no variation in the returns or standard deviation. The lesson: having these two funds in your portfolio will not reduce your investment risk.

Negative Correlation

With perfect negative correlation, the funds' returns move opposite to each other. If one fund has a positive return, you can anticipate that the other fund will have a negative return. This is illustrated in Table 4.2, showing that when one fund's return is high, the other's is correspondingly low.

In Table 4.2, hypothetical funds A and C are perfectly correlated negatively and have the same return (10 percent) and the same standard deviation (23 percent). But when combined into portfolio AC, deviations around their 10 percent returns cancel out. This means that with the hypothetical AC portfolio you can achieve the target return of 10 percent while eliminating the risk, as indicated by the 0 percent standard deviation.

Table 4.2   Negatively Correlated Funds

Year	Fund A	Fund C	Portfolio AC
1	32%	−12%	10%
2	−11%	31%	10%
3	−14%	34%	10%
4	33%	−13%	10%
5	−8%	28%	10%
6	28%	−9%	10%
Average return	10%	10%	10%
Standard deviation	23%	23%	0%

Reprinted with permission from TIAA-CREF's *Advance* magazine, June 2006 issue.

Zero Correlation

With zero correlation, there's no relationship between the returns of the selected securities. As a result, the returns of one security are not an indicator of the returns of another. For this reason, we don't include a table with zero correlated funds.

Correlation and Diversification

Because investors use correlation to improve diversification, the important question is: When can diversification help a portfolio by reducing risk?

- When you combine two or more funds with perfect positive correlation, there's no reduction of portfolio risk. The risk of the resulting portfolio is simply an average of the individual risks of the two funds. If you add more funds, or securities, with perfect positive correlation, the portfolio will continue to produce an average return without reducing risk. Such an allocation would not help reduce your portfolio risk;

- If you combine two or more funds that have zero correlation, portfolio risk may be reduced because the funds move independently and are statistically unrelated. If you add more uncorrelated funds or securities to the portfolio, you may be able to reduce risk, but not eliminate it completely. This allocation would help reduce your portfolio risk; or

- If you combine two or more funds with perfect negative correlation, you could eliminate risk altogether, which would be the ideal portfolio.

In the real world, extreme correlations such as those illustrated in Tables 4.1 and 4.2 are rare. Typically, securities have some positive correlation

Table 4.3   A Real-World Example

Year	Fund A	Fund D	Portfolio AD
1	32%	23%	28%
2	−11%	25%	7%
3	−14%	18%	2%
4	33%	17%	25%
5	−8%	−35%	−22%
6	28%	11%	20%
Average return	10%	10%	10%
Standard deviation	23%	23%	18%

Reprinted with permission from TIAA-CREF's *Advance* magazine, June 2006 issue.

with each other because investment markets are generally interrelated. Ideally, you'd like to set up a portfolio that is negatively correlated or with very low positive correlation.

Table 4.3 illustrates the more likely real-world scenario of positively correlated hypothetical funds A and D, which have identical standard deviations of 23 percent and average returns of 10 percent separately. When these funds are combined into portfolio AD, portfolio risk is reduced, as indicated by the lower 18 percent standard deviation. This would be a worthwhile allocation because it would give you the targeted 10 percent return while lowering portfolio risk from 23 percent to 18 percent.

All in all, "These simple hypothetical examples show that by diversifying among a few assets that behave differently, you can improve your portfolio by reducing its overall risk," says Govia. Bond funds tend to correlate negatively with stock funds, for example, while guaranteed accounts and real estate accounts have little or no correlation with each other or any other asset class.

To learn more about asset allocation and diversification, go to the Asset Allocation Evaluator in the "Calculators and Planning Tools" section of the TIAA-CREF Website, www.tiaa-cref.org.

Reprinted with permission from TIAA-CREF's *Advance* magazine, June 2006 issue.

Chapter 5

Planning for Retirement

It is commonly agreed that most individuals calculating how much to save during their working years should expect that they will need to replace 70 percent to 80 percent of their preretirement income. However, considering that longevity is increasing, it is surprising that future retirees are not saving as much as they will need during retirement years. Hewitt Associates, in a study of 2.6 million Americans eligible for a 401(k) or other defined-contribution (DC) plan, indicated that 72 percent were putting their money into a 401(k), and 81 percent had a separate retirement savings account. However, the company found a disparity of expectations about retirement funding between different generations of savers (Table 5.1). The study also found that Americans were not saving enough for retirement: the median balance in a 401(k) was only $27,100 ($40,730 for men and $18,130 for women). In addition, one-third of employees eligible for a 401(k) did not participate in the program.[1] Experts observe that although physicians as a group put away more for retirement than the average American, their savings may still fall well short of what they will need to fund a comfortable retirement.[2]

There is a broad consensus that personal savings and retirement plans should be the major source of income during retirement rather than Social Security. In planning for retirement, most physicians should consider four possible sources of income:

- **Personal savings.** Fund that can be built up and invested during working years. These funds are self-directed and the amounts available will depend on the person's discipline, and savings and investment philosophy;

- **Pensions.** Cash accumulations or guaranteed annuity payments created by an employer/sponsor for a participant to withdraw benefits from at retirement or disability;

- **Personal pension plans.** Account that the self-employed or small-business owners can create for retirement savings; and

Table 5.1   Retirement Patterns for Three Generations

	Baby Boomers (1943–1964)	Gen X (1965–1980)	Gen Y (1981–2000)
DC plan participation rate	72%	63.1%	31.3%
Rate of contribution	8.3%	7.2%	5.6%
Average total plan balance	$93,190	$31,240	$3,200
On track to replace DC plan and Social Security income	88.4%	44.1%	43%
Means of support during retirement			
Company-sponsored retirement savings plan	91%	93%	92%
Pension plan	73%	66%	64%
Social Security	78%	60%	57%
Private investments	91%	96%	63%
What gets in the way of savings for retirement			
Day-to-day expenses	67%		
Savings for children		53%	

Adapted from Hewitt Associates.

- **Social Security Insurance (SSI).** A government program that provides retirement benefits, disability credits, benefits for survivors, and credits for Medicare eligibility.

Pension Plans

Regulatory Requirements of Pension Plans

Pension plans are an important source of retirement income and are basically of two different varieties as discussed below.

Qualified Plans

These plans meet ERISA (Employee Retirement Income Security Act of 1974) requirements and are covered under IRS regulations for tax benefits. ERISA is a federal law passed by Congress that sets minimum standards for retirement plans in the private sector. ERISA rules currently do not cover federal, state, or local government plans, or certain church-associated plans. In addition, state worker's compensation plans and disability insurance laws are specifically excluded from ERISA.

ERISA laws cover standards ranging from spousal benefits, plan eligibility, and fiduciary accountability to vesting time. ERISA also requires plan administrators to give participants written notification on a regular basis about the details of the plan and a contact where further information may be available. ERISA does not mandate a retirement plan for employer/sponsors or how much of a benefit a participant must be paid. It simply sets minimum standards if a company does set up a pension plan. Any income generated within these accounts is non-taxable. Any contributions made by the employer/sponsor are tax deductible. Taxes are paid by the participant or the beneficiaries when there are withdrawals, and beneficiaries are accorded certain special tax advantages.

Non-Qualified Plans

These plans can be used in addition to profit sharing and other types of qualified plans. These plans are usually less expensive and customized to handle deferred compensation for highly paid executives. They do not meet all the ERISA requirements, and therefore, do not receive the same tax advantages.

Types of Pension Plan by Design

In general, pension plans are divided into defined benefit (DB), defined contribution (DC), or hybrid plans.

Defined-Benefit Pension Plans

There are two types of DB plans. The first type provides a guaranteed interest rate on employer contributions leading up to retirement, and the account value at the end is annuitized. This type of DB plan results in lower monthly payments and carries much less risk for the employer. The second type of DB plan guarantees a monthly retirement payment, which is discussed here.

As the name suggests, a DB plan is designed to produce a defined benefit or annual pension amount paid out after retirement. An actuary calculates the future benefits based on the current age, projected retirement age, expected mortality rates, expected annual salary, and projected investment returns during and following retirement. As an example, a company may have a DB plan that will pay a retiring participant $250 per month for every year worked. The benefit may or may not be linked to inflation and may be a final average plan, where the average salary of the last five years of employment is used to calculate the monthly payout.

Unlike DC plans, where a maximum contribution by the employer of $45,000 per participant or 100 percent of compensation (whichever is less) in 2007 is allowed for individuals under age 50, larger tax-deductible contributions can be made in a DB pension plan. For 2007, the annual benefit for a participant under a DB plan cannot exceed the lesser of the

Figure 5.1   DB Plans at a Glance

- Significant benefits are possible in a relatively short period of time.

- Employers can contribute (and deduct) more than under other retirement plans.

- Plan provides a predictable benefit that cannot be retroactively decreased.

- Plan can be used to promote certain business strategies by offering subsidized early retirement benefits.

- Plan is administratively complex and costly.

- Excise tax applies if the minimum contribution requirement is not satisfied.

- Vesting can be immediate or spread out over a seven-year period.

- Benefits are not dependent on asset returns.

- Other retirement plans can be made available.

- Plan can be used in businesses of any size.

Source: www.pbgc.gov (accessed May 10, 2006).

following amounts: 100 percent of the participant's average compensation for his/her highest three consecutive calendar years of participation or $180,000. See Figure 5.1 for DB plans at a glance.

Advantages of DB Plans

DB plans are ideal for physicians who have worked for a few years, reached their peak earning power, have a reasonably steady source of income, plan to continue working for a minimum of five years, and do not have many highly paid participants in the plan.[3] Additional benefits for the plan participant are:

- **Large contributions.** DB plans allow the largest contributions to be made;

- **Reduced risk.** The employer/sponsor bears the risk of uncertain markets, because the participant is usually paid in the form of annuity;

- **Security.** The employer/sponsor funds the plan and the benefits are known ahead of time, based on a set formula; and

- **Adjustments for cost of living.** Few of the remaining, successful DB plans have cost-of-living adjustments (COLA). Those that do may be underfunded. With COLA features, the retiree has less worry that the pension payments will fall behind the rate of inflation.

Disadvantages of DB Plans

These plans have several drawbacks compared with other pension options and have been falling out of favor with employer/sponsors for several years. These drawbacks are discussed in the following sections.

Complicated rules. Most employees and some employer/sponsors find the rules hard to understand.

Workforce issues. Because the law requires the same contributions for full-time employees, the plan becomes expensive if the practice has a large number of full-time, highly paid employees. The cost of the DB plan increases as the workforce ages. This is because of the J-shaped accrual rate. This means that benefits grow slowly at a young age, but as employees get closer to retirement, the employer/sponsor must contribute more for the older worker to guarantee the benefit promised.[4]

Minimum contribution rules. The employer/sponsor must make sufficient annual contributions, otherwise there is the potential that the tax-deductible status may be disallowed and penalties imposed. This particular risk has resulted in a sharp decline in the number of employers that offer a DB plan, and makes these plans better suited for large employers, such as public sector entities, that have a relatively stable population. Fewer than 1 in 10 physicians today are covered by these plans.[2] Even if an expert is making the actuarial calculations, the vagaries of unknown longevity, and uncertain market performance can make the DB plan a risk that most companies do not want to take. In addition, because contributions come directly from earnings, the bottom-line is affected. Major companies (for example, IBM, Verizon, and Motorola) have frozen their DB plans and pushed employee-funded DC plans instead.

Regulatory requirements. Rules set by the Pension Benefit Guaranty Corporation (PBGC) must be followed to ensure there are enough reserves to accommodate a bankruptcy of the employer/sponsor. PBGC is a government agency that insures private-sector pension plans and was created by ERISA. It is funded by insurance premiums paid by approximately 30,000 sponsors of various private pension plans that cover more than 44 million U.S. citizens.[5] Recent bankruptcies of airlines and other large companies have revealed underfunding of pension plans. In these cases, responsibility for the pension plan is shifted to PBGC—that is, the taxpayer. The PBGC itself is in debt for more than $22 billion, and estimates that private pensions are underfunded by almost $450 billion.

Expense. DB plans may be more expensive to set up, fund, and administer than DC plans, such as 401(k) plans.

Lack of participant input. Decisions regarding investments are made by the DB plan's trustees (who are appointed by the plan owner), and not the individual participant.

Nonportability. Because of the actuarial complexity of placing a value on the transfer value, portability of the plan to another employer can be a problem for participants. This represents a disadvantage for employees who leave a company offering one of these plans prior to retirement.

Defined-Contribution Plans

In contrast to the DB plan, the contribution made to the defined plan is defined or specified, but the benefit at retirement is not known. DC plans account for the majority of pension plans in the United States at this time. DC plans include: 401(k), 403(b), employee stock ownership plans (ESOPs), and profit-sharing plans.

Who Contributes?

A DC plan is a relatively inexpensive, recurrent benefit provided by an employer. In addition to participants deferring their salaries into a DC plan, an employer/sponsor can be the sole contributor, or can match participants' contributions. The sponsor can then arrange for the contributions to be invested and the cumulative amount at retirement for that participant is the result of the contributions, in addition to expenses and any gains or losses incurred over time.

Maximum Tax-Deferred Amounts

In 2007, the account of a participant cannot exceed the lesser of the following amounts: 100 percent of the participant's compensation, or $45,000 a year plus $5,000 for employees over the age of 50 as a "catch-up" amount. This is in contrast to the more generous limits in a DB plan, as previously mentioned.

Withdrawal Rules

With some exceptions, withdrawals can begin at age 59½. Lump-sum withdrawals can be eligible for 10-year averaging. A word of caution about lump sum withdrawals of pension contributions: You should check with the plan sponsor to ensure that withdrawal does not exclude you from retiree benefits such as health insurance.

Advantages of DC Plans

These plans have many positives, including:

- Easier to understand than a DB plan;

- Easier to promote savings habits through tax-deferral and automatic-payroll deductions;

- Less risk for employer/sponsors, though more for employees. The employee assumes the risks associated with the investments and chooses the asset allocation. However, there is a fiduciary responsibility attached to the employer/sponsor to educate employees (not advise them), even though the employee makes the decisions and has control over the assets; and

- Easier to transfer when the employee moves because the actuarial costs are lower. Also, the plan is easier to maintain for the employer/sponsor because there is no need to estimate future benefits.

Disadvantages of DC Plans

These plans also have negatives (for employees), including:

- More risk for the employee. The employee assumes the risks associated with the investments;

- Harder for late entrants to build a sufficient sum in a short period of time;

- Limits on contributions. Tax-deferred contributions to DC plans are limited according to Section 415 of the Internal Revenue Code; and

- No guaranteed benefits. Because there are no guaranteed benefits at the end, there is a risk that the employee may run short of money by either outliving the savings or making bad investment decisions.

Contributions by an employer/sponsor can be made to both a DC and a DB plan if least one employee is covered by both plans. However, the tax deduction for those contributions is limited.

Keogh Plans

Keogh plans are designed to allow the self-employed, those who have part-time side jobs, and partnerships to have a vehicle for funding a retirement plan. The rules are similar to other retirement plans and boilerplate plans are available in most cases. Keogh plans have, for the most part, fallen by the wayside with the popularity of more recently available plans.

401(k) Plans

This popular savings plan for retirement (named after a section of the IRS Code of 1978) allows an employee to defer, before taxes, a part of their salary into a retirement account. The employer/sponsor may try to create an incentive for employees to contribute to their retirement by matching a part of the employee contribution.

Some points to consider regarding 401(k) plans:

- They are protected by ERISA pension laws;

- Under the 2006 Pension Protection Act, 401(k) plans now offer flexibility in naming beneficiaries and a choice of investment vehicles;

- Unlike IRAs, 401(k) plans allow limited withdrawals without a penalty if retirement is earlier than age 59½ (for example, if one separates from service at age 55 or older, has a disability, or medical expenses under certain conditions);

- 401(k)s allow a maximum deferral amount of $15,500 in 2007. There is a catch-up provision for those over age 50 to defer another $5,000 annually. There are certain cases when an individual may not be eligible to defer the full amount. One instance is when the company is limited in deferring the contribution for highly paid employees (more than $100,000 in 2007), if lower-paid employees are not eligible to participate based on a formula. The plan may become top-heavy because lower-paid employees do not contribute at all or too little;

- A 401(k) may allow withdrawals prior to retirement in circumstances where there is a hardship. To qualify as a hardship, the IRS requires that the need must be immediate and a heavy financial obligation that cannot be satisfied by other resources;

- Borrowing is permitted from the 401(k), unlike an IRA; and

- 401(k)s provide protection from creditors for qualified retirement plans like 401(k) and 403(b) plans.

Employer/sponsor's efforts to automatically enroll employees, simplify choices, and provide better education regarding the plans have resulted in greater participation. A recent study by Hewitt Associates, a human-resources outsourcing and consulting company, showed that 36 percent of employees hired within one year had participated in a 401(k) plan.[6] However, almost half of the employees either did not participate, or did not put enough into the plan to qualify for company matching. Better education of employees about asset allocation was shown to have increased the number of employees holding more than four investments from 40 percent in 2004 to 44 percent in 2005.

Employee Stock Ownership Plans (ESOP)

ESOPs are designed to encourage employees to invest their retirement contributions in company ownership by allowing investments in the form of company stock. For employers, the plan is inexpensive (stock comes from treasury stock) and gives the owners a selling market.

Profit-Sharing Plans

A profit-sharing plan allows the company to determine the amount, if any, that will be contributed to the employee's account based on profit or other measurement based on a formula, on an annual basis. A profit-sharing plan does not need to establish a definite formula for any profits to be shared. However, in the absence of a formula there must be systemic and substantial contributions. There is more flexibility in making contributions to this type of plan, rather than a DB or DC plan.

Individual Retirement Accounts (IRAs)

The U.S population has about $3.5 trillion dollars in IRAs and that amount is about 27 percent of the nation's $13 trillion in retirement savings.[7] IRAs are personal retirement savings accounts that receive favored tax considerations because all earnings are tax-deferred in the account until distribution. IRA contributions can only be made if one has taxable income such as wages, commissions, self-employment income, and payments from alimony or separation agreements. The IRS (as stated in its Publication 590) does not consider the following sources as compensation:

- Earnings and profits from property, such as rental income, interest income, and dividend income;

- Pension or annuity income;

- Deferred compensation received (compensation payments postponed from a past year);

- Income from a partnership for which no services were provided that constituted a material-income producing factor; and

- Any amounts excluded from income, such as foreign-earned income and housing costs.

The federal tax laws with regard to IRAs seem to change yearly and more types of IRAs have been added to the mix in recent years.

Table 5.2   Annual Limits for Contributions for 2007

DC plan contribution limit	$45,000
DB plan contribution limit	$180,000
401(k), 403(b), 457(b) contribution limit	$15,500
IRA contribution limit	$4,000
Catch-up contribution limit for 401(k), 403(b), 457(b)	$5,000
Catch-up contribution limit for IRA	$1,000

Source: www.irs.gov/retirement/article/0,,id=96461,00.html (accessed 3/8/2007).

Questions and Answers About IRAs

IRA accounts are essentially trust/custodial accounts through a bank/brokerage or other financial institution. Here are answers to common questions about IRAs.

How Much Can I Put in an IRA? The annual contribution limit will be increased from $4,000 currently to $5,000 in 2008 and will be indexed for inflation in the future. In addition, the catch-up amount for persons over age 50 has increased to $1,000 per year after 2005 (Table 5.2). Funds invested in an IRA must be from compensation and not another retirement account's portfolio income or from deferred compensation. There is a 6-percent penalty for putting in more than the legally allowed amount.

Is the Contribution to an IRA Tax Deductible? This depends on the income level and whether the contributor or spouse is covered by another retirement plan. For 2007, if covered by a retirement plan at work, the deduction for contributions to a traditional IRA will be reduced (phased out) if the modified adjusted gross income (AGI) is:

- More than $83,000 but less than $103,000 for a married couple filing a joint return, or a qualifying widow(er);

- More than $52,000 but less than $62,000 for a single individual or head of household; or

- Less than $10,000 for a married individual filing a separate return.

What Are the Options for IRA Withdrawals? In general IRA withdrawal options depend on the needs of the participant. They can be based on a percentage of assets (fixed) or dollar-adjusted (withdrawal adjusted according to inflation). The former method is likely to last through retirement years, and imposes more discipline on spending. However, it may be prone to fluctuations depending on the performance of the portfolio and spending patterns. The dollar-adjusted method is adjusted for inflation and is more predictable. With both methods, constant re-evaluation in view of inflation, performance of the portfolio, and spending is necessary.

If the contribution is tax deductible, ordinary income tax rates apply upon withdrawal on both the contributions and earnings. If the contribution was made with after-tax dollars, only the earnings are taxed at ordinary income tax rates. One can, however, choose to not take a deduction for an IRA contribution and receive the withdrawals tax free. One is required to start withdrawing regular IRA funds at age 70½ (following April 1 of the year after you turn 70½). However, in some cases, if one's tax bracket is going to be lower soon after retirement, say at age 65, and the bracket is expected to increase at age 71 for some reason, it is obviously prudent to start making some withdrawals earlier than age 70½.

The most common misunderstanding is that an IRA holder cannot take any withdrawals until age 59½. There are several circumstances that allow for early withdrawals:

- The so-called 72(t) payments (by the tax code) allow a person to withdraw a "series of substantially equal periodic payments" on a schedule before age 59½ and avoid the 10-percent penalty for early withdrawal. For instance, if an IRA holder starts withdrawing money from an IRA at age 53, he/she would have to continue taking payments for at least five years or until age 59½, whichever is longer. If an IRA holder starts at age 56, then payments would continue till age 61. Once payments are taken, say at age 59½, they can be changed one time; or

- If the funds are used to pay medical expenses. Medical expenses can be paid if the expenses exceed 7.5 percent of AGI or certain other situations such as educational expenses or unemployment. The penalties on every year of pre-59½ age withdrawal, plus interest on the withdrawals, add up. Expert accounting and financial advice is needed to calculate withdrawing IRA money and to take into account the tax bracket one anticipates being in later.

How Is an Inherited IRA Handled? An inherited IRA may be transferred from one custodian (bank or brokerage firm) that has to permit such a transfer to another by a direct rollover without the beneficiary actually handling the money. They are frequently called *stretch* IRAs due to the tax benefits being stretched out over a long time. A *conduit* IRA is a separate IRA established for a rollover into a qualified employer-sponsored plan. Withdrawals may be taken over the life expectancy of the beneficiary; the first withdrawal must be taken by the end of the calendar year following the owner's demise. The younger the beneficiary, the more money can grow tax deferred in the IRA as the required distributions are smaller.

IRA Rollovers A *rollover* implies that a person is taking a tax-free distribution of the retirement plan and rolling it over into another form of retirement plan within a specified time period. If monies are simply transferred from one trustee to another, no waiting period is necessitated and the transfer is not taxable. A common error is to improperly roll over a previous 401(k) or another pension-plan account, or even change financial institutions.

A rollover must be completed by the 60th day following the day on which a distribution is received (to avoid a 10-percent penalty). The 60-day period can be extended for the period during which the distribution is in a frozen deposit in a financial institution. The IRS may also waive the 60-day requirement where "failure to do so would be against equity or good conscience, such as in the event of a casualty, disaster, or other event beyond your reasonable control."[8] An appeal to the IRS usually results in avoidance of paying taxes on the entire amount of the transfer (automatic waiver), but it behooves one to monitor the paperwork to make sure the financial institution or bank has followed through and the time deadline has not expired.

Having a legally valid will does not mean that one does not have to fill out the beneficiary form correctly. A copy of the beneficiary form should be in the IRA holder's file because when circumstances and financial plans change, a new beneficiary form may have to be filled out. Usually, the beneficiary of an IRA is a spouse, not an estate. An IRA beneficiary takes precedence over a will. If no beneficiary is named for an IRA account and the estate is the beneficiary, the stretch options are lost and distributions are required. Upon distributions, the funds can be subject to creditors claims because they are no longer in an IRA. An overall estate plan will take into account all the financial circumstances and tax laws, and allow the legal advisor to make the will consistent with other instruments that control the financial assets. A trust tax rate is generally higher than individual rates, and stretched out withdrawals over time that allow assets to grow tax free may be disallowed for various reasons.

IRAs and Bankruptcy Protection Until recently, each state had different laws with regard to protection of IRA assets from creditors in case of bankruptcy. The U.S. Supreme Court recently ruled that federal bankruptcy protections are now available not only for ERISA-covered employer-sponsored plans, i.e., 403(b) and 401(k), but also for non-employer-sponsored plans including IRAs (not Roth IRAs), education savings accounts, and college savings accounts (529 plans). There is some ambiguity, as the Court ruled that the protection is limited to the "amount reasonably necessary for the support of the debtor and any dependent," which could make some portion of the assets vulnerable. As part of a broader bankruptcy law passed by Congress and signed by President Bush, as of Oct. 1, 2005, up to $1 million in IRA contributions and earnings are protected from creditors, in addition to amounts rolled over into an IRA from previous retirement plans.

Roth IRA

Named for former Senate Finance Committee Chairman William Roth of Delaware, a Roth IRA does not give tax-deductible status to contributions as does a traditional IRA (Table 5.3), but savers can exclude withdrawals from taxes, including those from income accrued in the account.

Table 5.3   Comparison of Traditional and Roth IRAs

Feature	Regular IRA	Roth IRA
Age limit	Contributions not allowed after age 70½	No age limit
Contribution limit	$4,000 for 2006 and 2007 plus $1,000 catch-up for persons over age 50; $5,000 starting in 2008 and increase of $500 increments	$4,000 for 2006 and 2007 plus $1,000 catch-up for persons over age 50; $5,000 starting in 2008 and increase of $500 increments
Tax deductible	Usually not, exceptions exist	No
Income cap	None	Yes
Tax consequences of earnings	Tax deferred. Any earnings are added to regular taxable income.	Tax deferred
Tax consequences of distribution	Taxed as ordinary income	Distributions are tax-free
Tax consequences of early withdrawal	Penalty on early withdrawal if age <59½	Distributions may be taken anytime, no penalty for qualified withdrawals
Required minimum distribution rules for owners	Owners required to start distributing minimum amounts beginning April 1 of the year after the year in which they reach age 70½	None
Required minimum distribution rules for beneficiaries	Same as owners	Required to comply with minimum distribution rules

No contributions to a Roth IRA for 2007 are allowed if:

- Income exceeds $166,000 (modified AGI), and if the IRA holder is married and files a joint tax return; or

- Annual income exceeds $114,000 and if the IRA holder files as single, head of household, or married-filing-separately and did not live with his/her spouse at any time during the tax year. A partial contribution is allowed for those with AGI between $95,000 and $110,000.

Roth IRA Withdrawal Rules

Withdrawals from Roth IRAs can be made under certain conditions, including:

- At least five years have passed after opening the IRA and after attaining age 59½;

- Disability;

- Purchase of a home (lifetime limit of $10,000); or

- Beneficiary receiving the distribution after the Roth IRA holder's death.

In addition, withdrawal is allowed if the distributions are taken no earlier than five years (beginning with the tax year in which the first contribution was made) after the taxpayer funds his/her first Roth IRA.

For individuals who seek an advantage with a Roth IRA, in addition to other restrictions, a regular IRA can be converted to a Roth only if the AGI is less than $100,000 and all converted amount is taxed at current tax rates. However, Congress recently passed the Tax Reconciliation Act, which eliminates the $100,000 AGI ceiling for converting a traditional IRA to a Roth IRA, for tax years after 2009. The conversion will be treated as a taxable distribution, but will not be subject to the 10 percent early withdrawal penalty. Taxpayers who convert from a traditional IRA to a Roth IRA in 2010 may elect to recognize the conversion income in 2010, or average it over the next two years.

If the Tax Reconciliation Act is still in force in 2010, how can one get ready to take advantage of that future benefit today? The new act also permits a non-deductible IRA for individuals under age 70½ with any taxable compensation. There is no tax deduction for the contribution; taxes are deferred on investment income until withdrawal of the funds. A non-deductible IRA account can have a maximum of $8,000 annually for married couples filing jointly. The amount can then be converted into a Roth IRA in 2010. However, taxes will be due on the investment income upon conversion and planning for this ahead of time is necessary. Critics of the Tax Reconciliation Act point out that although this provides short-term, additional revenue to the U.S. Treasury because taxes will be paid on the fair market value of the dollars being converted from an IRA to a Roth IRA, it may be a wash in the long term. If tax rates go up, individuals in higher-income brackets will benefit by paying taxes on the conversion in 2010, and paying no taxes on the withdrawal from the Roth IRA at a time when they may be in an even higher-tax bracket. The primary beneficiaries appear to be higher-income individuals, but a careful analysis of each situation is warranted.

Choosing Between a 401(k) and a Roth IRA

If only one could predict what the income-tax rates would be on retirement! All tax-deferred retirement plans are just that: deferred tax at the ordinary rate. If the contributor's current tax bracket is high now and projected to be lower at retirement, the IRA would be a better choice simply because taxes are deferred and paid at a lower rate on withdrawal. Conversely, if taxes rates increase, contributors to a Roth IRA would have paid taxes at a lower tax rate and withdrawals later would be non-taxable. Congress could just as easily make part of the earnings in a Roth IRA taxable in the future. Some advocate a hedging tactic. Because it is required that the contributor withdraw money from a 401(k) or a regular IRA at age 70½ (required minimum distribution), that may put him/her into a higher tax bracket. If eligible, one could contribute to a company IRA up to a level where the company stops matching your contribution, at which time the rest is placed in a Roth IRA until the point where the amount contributed to it starts phasing out.

Multiple Employer-Sponsored Retirement Plans

The contribution limits for deferral of salary are meant for individuals rather than per plan. Regardless of the number of tax-deferred plans, the individual limit for employees is indicated in Table 5.2. If one has two employers/sponsors and wishes to defer salary from both, the total amount for both plans is still $15,500 in 2007 plus the catch-up provision.

The employer/sponsor may have a DC plan referred to as an *annual-addition plan*, where the contribution made on behalf of the employee is limited to the lesser of $45,000 for 2007 (a $1,000 increase for inflation is periodically announced by the IRS) or 100 percent of compensation. This limit is for all contributions to multiple plans within the company sponsoring the retirement plan. If there is yet another employer/sponsor, one can have another annual-addition plan with the same limit, unless the businesses are linked in some fashion. As an example, if a physician is paid a salary of $300,000 annually from his/her private practice, the total amount including 401(k), profit sharing, and matching funds by the employer/sponsor can be an aggregate of $45,000 for 2007. If the physician is also employed by a hospital for consulting activities and is eligible to contribute, additional contributions can be made to a 403(b) and a 457(b) plan.

Pre-tax salary deferrals to 457(b) plans are not considered deferrals by the IRS. This means that if the employer/sponsor has both 403(b) and 457(b) plans (typically those are found at state teaching institutions), each has a limit of $15,500. In addition to this is the catch-up amount for 2007, provided the total amount in each plan does not exceed 100 percent of the individual's compensation.

Simplified Employee Pension Plans (SEPs)

SEPs are employer-sponsored retirement plans with relatively minimal reporting requirements that allow employees to receive tax-deferred contributions to their IRAs. These plans are not covered by ERISA and are usually established by someone who is a sole proprietor, in a partnership, or a business owner (of either an unincorporated or incorporated business, including subchapter S corporations); and has any self-employed income by providing a service, either full time or part time. They could, however, be subject to creditors claims.

Supplemental Retirement Plans: 403(b)s and 457(b)s

Supplemental retirement plans are voluntary savings plans that allow employees to have a certain amount (which can be changed) deducted from their paycheck. Savings are then allowed to accumulate tax-free until withdrawal. If death occurs while working, the savings are passed on to the designated beneficiary. A 403(b) retirement plan is usually offered by a not-for-profit or tax-exempt organization and a 457(b) DC plan is available from a state or local government. These plans are so named because of the IRS code under which they are mentioned. State universities and public-school teachers are often eligible for both plans. These plans are meant to supplement pension plans and Social Security payments. They are considered pre-tax, meaning that the contributions will result in lower-taxable income and before any federal taxes are calculated.

Annual contribution limits to each plan have been raised to $15,500 in 2007. After 2007, contribution limits will be increased based on the cost of living and in increments of $500 annually. An employee under age 50 can potentially contribute a total of up to $31,000 a year (pre-tax) to both plans till 2007. Under catch-up provisions, people over the age of 50 (or those within three years of normal retirement) can save up to a total $41,000 in both 403(b) and 457(b) plans. Most supplemental retirement plans have loan provisions.

In 403(b) plans, annuities and mutual funds may be the only investment option and because the contributions are made pre-tax, it may make sense if the fees are reasonably low. The triggering event for withdrawal from a 403(b) plan may be reaching age 59½ , separation from service, death, disability, or financial hardship.

The 457(b) plans are non-qualified and are not covered under ERISA. Contributions to 457(b) plans are made pre-tax and any withdrawals before age 59½ can be made without the 10-percent penalty (unlike the 403(b) plan). The 457(b) plans are generally required to have low operating fees and offer low-cost mutual funds. If the employee leaves the employer/sponsor (usually the reason), retires, reaches the age of 70½, dies, or encounters an unforeseen emergency (under IRS Section 457), the funds are available to be used. The emergency may be an unexpected illness of the employee or dependent, or significant property loss that is unexpected and imposes severe financial circumstances. Debt, divorce, or tuition expenses are not considered unforeseen emergencies by the IRS. Ordinary income taxes are paid on any withdrawals.

Funds in a 457(b) plan will lose their special status if rolled over into a non-457(b) account and may be subject to the 10-percent penalty if withdrawn before age 59½ . On the other hand, a non-457(b) account rolled into a 457(b) simply has to be tracked and accounted for separately to avoid triggering the 10-percent early withdrawal penalty.

Annuities

Annuities are among the largest retirement vehicles (almost $2 billion) next to 401(k) IRAs (over $2.2 billion).[9] *Annuity* is a general term for retirement funding vehicles and is an insurance contract that essentially enables a client to pay an insurance carrier either a lump sum or payments (accumulated tax-free). In return, the company guarantees the client a regular stream of income per month/year for a specified period of time. There are two types of annuities: fixed or variable. Fixed annuities have an underlying interest rate tied to the premium payment. Variable annuities are subject to the value of the performance of sub-accounts managed by professional managers.

Annuity Options

There are several kinds of annuitization options available. Both the fixed and variable annuities can be immediate or deferred, including:

- **One-life.** Pays only one person with payments ending at death. A two-life annuity pays less than a one-life, but payments will continue to the surviving partner;

- **Fixed-period.** Pays out entire accumulation over a specified number of years;

- **Transfer-payout.** Allows cash withdrawals from a traditional annuity plan in about 10 equal payments;

- **Single-sum.** Full or partial cash distributions with some surrender charges and fees; and

- **Systematic-withdrawal.** The recipient withdraws specified amounts— either a lump sum or a series of regular periodic payments—on a predetermined frequency until the account is emptied.

Advantages of Annuities

There are several positives related to annuities:

- There are living and death benefits. Guarantees, however, are only as good as the insurance company providing the benefits;

- Funds accumulate tax-free;

- Recent annuities (stripped-down versions) can be being bought with no initial load fees, at much lower costs, and without penalties (exit charges) for changing to another annuity; and

- They provide asset protection from creditor claims.

Disadvantages of Annuities

There are several negatives related to annuities, including:

- Surrender charges are usually incurred for withdrawal sooner than about seven years;

- For non-qualified withdrawals prior to age 59½, there is a penalty of 10 percent and ordinary income tax on gains only;

- Contracts are difficult to understand, particularly when all the different "bells and whistles" are considered;

- Fees may include insurance costs and large administrative charges (the average fees are about 2.34 percent compared with mutual fund fees of 1.42 percent annually).[9] Because the insurance company is bearing the market risk for any guarantees, the fees are necessarily greater than for a mutual fund;

- Switching annuities is usually associated with penalties. Buyers must compare the penalties with recent decreases in fees and expenses to calculate a break-even point and decide if the switch is worth it;

- There is no "step-up" upon death and substantial taxes may be due at ordinary income-tax rates;

- Annuities are not Federal Deposit Insurance Corporation (FDIC) insured; and

- Variable and indexed annuities may have certain charges fixed for a period of time, with penalties and unintended tax implications.

Social Security Insurance

The Social Security Administration reports that in 2006 Social Security Insurance (SSI) benefits were paid to about 48 million people. Those benefits accounted for nearly 40 percent of income for the average retiree. Almost two-thirds of all SSI benefits go to retirees; 18.4 percent for survivor benefits (widows/widowers/children) of beneficiaries; 13 percent to disabled workers; and 5.8 percent to spouses.[10]

The exact amount of the benefit depends on the birth year, retirement age, and the annual income reported over a working life. In most cases, a worker needs to earn 40 credits (or 10 years of working), to be eligible for SSI benefits. The Social Security Administration distributes an annual statement explaining retirement benefits, disability credits, benefits for survivors, and credits for Medicare eligibility.[10,11] The monthly check is payment for the prior month and no payment is made for the month during which a beneficiary dies. Surviving spouses, dependent children, and parents financially dependent on the beneficiary who qualify, may be eligible for payment.

SSI Taxes

Since 1994, all earnings are taxed for Medicare purposes, whereas the wage base for SSI taxes is $97,500 for 2007. In 2007, a total of 12.4 percent for each worker is paid into SSI and 2.9 percent into Medicare (together called

Table 5.4   Social Security and Medicare Taxes in 2007

	Social Security Taxes 2007	Medicare Taxes 2007
Employer/employee (each)	6.2% on earnings up to $97,500	1.456% on all earnings
Self-employed	12.4% on earnings up to $97,500	2.9% on all earnings

NOTE: Self-employment taxes can be offset by income-tax provisions.

Source: www.ssa.gov/pubs/1003.pdf.

Federal Insurance Contribution Act [FICA] taxes). Half of the amount is paid by the employee (6.2 percent of salary up to $97,500 for 2007 in SSI taxes and 1.45 percent in Medicare taxes on the entire salary). The other half (6.2 percent in SSI taxes and 1.45 percent in Medicare taxes) is contributed by the employer/sponsor. Self-employed individuals pay the entire 12.4 percent in SSI taxes and 2.9 percent into the Medicare fund based on net earnings (Table 5.4). However, the self-employed can claim credit for half the tax on their income tax return.

SSI Benefits

Approximately one-third of SSI recipients pay income tax on their benefits. Up to 50 percent of the SSI benefit may be taxable if the sum of total taxable income (including wages, interest, and dividends or other income), plus tax-exempt interest, plus one-half of the SSI benefit is between $25,000 and $34,000 for a single filer or between $32,000 and $44,000 for a married couple filing jointly. If the sum exceeds $34,000 for a single filer or $44,000 for joint filers, up to 85 percent of the benefit may be taxable. Having a larger amount saved in a Roth IRA and paying some of the living expenses through Roth withdrawals (rather than taxable accounts or from pretax IRAs) may allow the retiree to stay below the $32,000 base amount and minimize taxes.

A spouse is entitled to a spousal benefit of half of the retiree's full benefit unless he/she has started collecting benefits prior to reaching full retirement age. If so, spousal benefits are permanently reduced by a percentage based on the number of months until full retirement age. Full benefits may be paid if the spouse has a child. Spousal benefits are not relevant if the person has worked enough to receive greater benefits based on their own work record. Social Security pays retirement benefits first, so that at death, retirement benefits are paid to the retiree's spouse and any spousal benefits are discontinued. If the retiree is divorced and the ex-spouse is age 62 or older, unmarried and the marriage lasted 10 years, the ex-spouse is eligible for benefits based on the retiree's SSI record. This does not affect the current spouse's benefits. At the retiree's death, the surviving spouse has to take into

Table 5.5   Effects of Retiring Later than SSI Retirement Age

Year of Birth	Yearly Percent Benefit Increase
1935–1936	6
1937–1938	6.50
1939–1940	7
1941–1942	7.50
1943 or later	8

account the total financial picture and consult with an experienced financial advisor to look at all sources of income, including life insurance.

Disabled persons can receive benefits after six months of disability if they have earned enough credits and a physical or mental impairment has occurred that is expected to prevent a claimant from doing substantial work for a year or more, or may result in death.

Availability of SSI Benefits

Application for benefits is made 3 months prior to receiving SSI payments. In 1983, the full retirement age was raised gradually from age 65 (born before 1937), to age 66 for people born before 1955, and to age 67 for people born after 1960. A detailed list of SSI eligibility ages is available at the Website, www.socialsecurity.gov. Retirement benefits may be taken early (at age 62), but at a reduced rate that is about 20 percent less than the full benefit. More details are available at www.socialsecurity.gov. In contrast, greater benefits are received if an individual continues to work past retirement age. If benefits are taken years before full retirement age, $1 in benefits is deducted for each $2 in earnings above the annual limit ($12,480 in 2006). If full retirement age is reached, any employment income does not affect SSI benefits. Earnings in this case apply to earned income, not interest or dividends. If retirees plan to work and have enough private income, they may wish to delay receiving SSI benefits. If the retiree was born before 1943, for every year that benefits are delayed, benefits increase by 8 percent per year until age 70 (Table 5.5). A meeting with a Social Security Administration official may be valuable about one year prior to applying for any benefits.

Spending in Retirement

Spending in retirement depends on the tax bracket and sources of income at the time. As an example, if the retiree is in the lowest income tax bracket, in some cases, it may make sense to withdraw funds from an IRA account first to the level of the next higher tax bracket. In general, of the various sources of funds available after retirement, most financial experts recommend spending from funds in the following order:

1. Regular after-tax savings account (taxable assets);

2. IRA and 401(k) accounts (tax-deferred assets); and

3. Roth IRA and Roth 401(k) accounts (tax free).

The reasoning is that one is required to start withdrawing a regular IRA after age 70½; the Roth IRA has no such requirement. Therefore, the Roth IRA can accumulate income while the other accounts are being spent. Inherited Roth IRAs are, however, subject to federal and state taxes for the heirs. For more information on estate taxes, see chapter 2, "Individual Coporate Taxation," in Volume 1 of The Smarter Physician Series (©2007 Medical Group Management Association).

References

1. Hewitt Associates LLC, "Three Generations Prepare for Retirement," February 2006, www.hewittassociates.com/_MetaBasicCMAssetCache_ /Assets/Articles/three_generations06.pdf) (accessed June 27, 2006).

2. K. McKee, "Physicians Need To Do More to Boost Their Retirement Plan Growth," *Medical Economics*, Aug. 19, 2005, www.memag.com/ memag/article/articleDetail.jsp?id=174467&pageID=1&sk=&date (accessed Oct. 16, 2006).

3. Wikipedia, "Pensions," Oct. 14, 2006, http://en.wikipedia.org/wiki/ pension (accessed Oct. 14, 2006).

4. Pension Benefit Guaranty Corporation, www.pbgc.gov (accessed May 10, 2006).

5. Internal Revenue Service, "Choosing a Retirement Plan: Defined Benefit Plan," United States Dept. of Treasury, www.irs.gov/retirement/ article/0,,id=108950,00.html (accessed June 27, 2006).

6. Hewitt Associates LLC, "Hewitt Study: Company Efforts Positively Impact U.S. Employees' 401(k) Savings Habits," May 16, 2006, http://www.hewittassociates.com/Intl/NA/en-US/AboutHewitt/ Newsroom/PressReleaseDetail.aspx?cid=2781 (accessed May 17, 2006).

7. K. Greene, "How Retirees Are Blowing Their Nest Eggs," *Wall Street J*, June 27 (2005): R1–3.

8. Internal Revenue Service, United States Dept. of Treasury, www.irs.gov (accessed May 10, 2006).

9. J.D. Opdyke, "Annuities Lighten Up," *Wall Street J*, May 13 (2006): B1.

10. Social Security Online, "Retirement: Plan Your Retirement," Social Security Administration, www.socialsecurity.gov (accessed May 10, 2006).

11. Social Security Online, "Information About Your Statement," Social Security Administration, www.socialsecurity.gov/mystatement (accessed May 10, 2006).

Additional Resources

Social Security Administration

- Telephone: 1.800.772.1213

- Have ready Social Security number, birth certificate, and proof of U.S. citizenship for those not born in the United States, W-2 forms for the last year, bank account name and number for a direct deposit.

- *The Appeals Process* (Publication No. 05-10041) and *Your Right to Representation* (Publication No. 05-10075).

Helpful Websites

Investopedia.com: www.investopedia.com/retirement.asp

Know Your Pension: www.knowyourpension.org

Useful Calculators

Use online calculators to compute compound interest in taxable and tax-free accounts, retirement savings targets and withdrawal amounts for Roth and traditional IRAs, annuities, and other retirement savings accounts.

A.G. Edwards & Sons, Inc.—www.agedwards.com

Moneychimp.com—www.moneychimp.com

TIAA-CREF—www.tiaa-cref.org

Time Value Software—www.tcalc.com

1728 Software Systems, Inc.—www.1728.com/annuity.htm

Vanguard Funds—www.vanguard.com

Chapter 6

Life Insurance: Tips for Buying It and Using It

Life insurance is part of a comprehensive estate plan to protect one's family. Life insurance can replace lost income, pay for a home mortgage, provide for educational support, cover loans and other debts, and can, if structured appropriately, offer tax advantages for beneficiaries. The most common reasons medical professionals considering purchasing a life insurance policy are to:

- Provide income for a non-working spouse or one with substantially less income;

- Support children or dependents with a disability or special need; and

- Pay off a home or other mortgage after the insured's death.

Insurance Terms

Some insurance terms to understand are:

- **Insurer.** Issues the legal contract, which specifies the terms and conditions of the life insurance policy and the risks assumed;

- **Insured.** The person whose life is insured, but not necessarily the owner of the policy;

- **Beneficiary.** The person or entity that will receive the proceeds from the insurance policy after the death of the insured. Unless the policy has an irrevocable beneficiary, the owner may choose to change the beneficiary;

- **Contestability period.** Usually two years within which the insurer can elect to challenge the claim and investigate it before paying or denying it. The usual proof of death is a death certificate and the insurance company's completed form, signed and notarized;

- **Maturation of the policy.** A policy is said to have matured when the insured dies, or reaches the age specified in the policy;

- **Face amount.** This is usually the amount paid by the insurance company when the policy matures; and

- **Rider.** An additional attachment or modification of the policy such as coverage for accidental death, waiver of premium, or guaranteed insurability.

How Insurance Companies Classify Health Status

Insurers of life insurance categorize a person's health status as one of the following:

- **Preferred best.** Applicant has no significant adverse medical history, is not on any medications, and there is no family history of diabetes, early cancer, or other serious conditions;

- **Preferred.** Similar to preferred best, except the applicant is taking medication for a condition and some family history is present; or

- **Standard.** Most applicants are in this category.

Term and Whole Life Insurance

There are two basic forms of life insurance: *term* and *whole life*, also called *cash value* (Table 6.1).

Term Life

In a term policy, the insurance company pays the beneficiary the death benefit if the insured dies while the policy is in effect. Term policies are meant to pay a death benefit and do not have any cash or investment value. This means that when the policy is discontinued or allowed to lapse, the premiums simply paid for the life protection. They are considerably cheaper than cash-value policies because the cost only reflects the insurance portion without the additional cash-value part. It is affordable for most young physicians starting out with no savings and with loans to pay off. Another time for purchasing this policy is if insurance protection is needed for a short time, such as prior to retirement or Social Security benefits. Most term policies are purchased for a specified but relatively shorter time frame (generally 5 years to 20 years), after which they will no longer pay the heirs.

There are various types of term insurance:

- annual renewable;

- level term;

- decreasing and increasing term; and

- mortgage insurance.

Most term policies are also *level term*, meaning the annual premium is fixed for the duration of the policy. An alternative is to purchase a policy where the initial premium is small at a younger age and then increases

Table 6.1   Comparison of Term and Whole Life Insurance Policies

	Term	Whole Life
Duration	Limited and specified	"Permanent" (death benefit and cash value)
Cash value (savings)	None	Savings accumulate; guaranteed cash value
Initial payments for same coverage	Significantly less than a whole life policy	Significantly more than a term life policy
Benefits	Only if death occurs during coverage period	Guaranteed coverage for life
Borrowing against cash value	No	Yes
Accelerated benefits option for terminal illness	Policy may offer	Policy may offer
Waiver of premium	Available	Available
Premiums	Same with level term, increase for annual renewable	Various depending on policy
Income-tax advantages	None	Yes
Investment returns	Can be significant *	Low
Evidence of insurability	On purchase (if over a certain amount) and for annual renewable policies	On purchase

* By investing the savings from buying a term policy instead of a whole life policy.

with age over the life of the policy. Annual renewable term policies allow for additional purchases, although with higher premiums.

The usual advice has been to purchase a term policy as a young, healthy person because of the low cost. A few years ago, rates for term policies were starting to go up partly due to regulations requiring insurance companies to have larger reserves available. However, premiums for term policies have dropped by about 50 percent over the past 10 years[1] because of longer life spans and increasing competition on the Internet. USAA Life Insurance reports that 5 years ago, a 40-year-old, non-smoking male would have paid $585 annually for a $500,000, 20-year term policy.[2] Currently, a 45-year-old male, non-smoker can get a replacement policy for the remaining 15 years for a 10-percent savings at approximately $525 annually.[2] If premiums on an older-level term policy seem expensive, it may be worth comparing prices with a new, lower-cost policy if no significant new illnesses have occurred and there is a continued need for insurance. *The Wall Street Journal* also reports that each year in age adds about 4 percent to 8 percent to the cost of term policies, with the sharpest increase at age 40.[2]

Whole Life (or Cash Value)

Whole life policies, also known as *cash-value policies*, come in many forms, are meant to be owned for life and essentially are level-term policies with a built-in savings component making them more expensive. The cost of a cash-value policy can be as much as four to eight times that of a term policy. This is partly because a large portion of the initial premium paid goes toward the sales commission and typically the policy does not accumulate much cash value in the first few years. If the premiums are not paid and the policy lapses during the first few years, all or most of the money is lost. The cash built up within the policy can be used during one's lifetime by either taking a loan against the policy (typically at a guaranteed rate), or "cashing out" by receiving the cash value while living. At the policyholder's death, the beneficiaries only get paid the face value (death benefit), not the face value and the cash value. A provision for receiving both is possible with higher premiums. The policy is suited for physicians who are otherwise not disciplined enough to save on a regular basis. There are some tax-advantage features that are not available to holders of term policies. Most experts argue that the difference in premium between term and cash-value policies can be invested with a better return over a long period of time without incurring the large initial commission and administrative cost of the latter. On a practical level, it takes discipline to put away a fixed amount every month.

Standard Cash-Value Policies

Standard cash-value policies guarantee level premiums, death benefits, and at least a minimum cash value. However, recent variations promise the possibility of greater cash value by investing the accumulated cash value in mutual funds—without emphasizing the fact that higher returns depend entirely on the investment returns obtained by the insurance company. If the investments are not successful, the greater cash values shown on any company brochures (other than listed as guaranteed) are not promised. Some policies also emphasize cash value over the death benefit, but fail to point out that by law all policies have to contain the death benefit. As a result, if there is no need for the death benefit, a better return on the amounts paid in premiums can be obtained by investing an equivalent amount without the administrative and insurance costs. There are many variations on the standard whole life (ordinary cash value) policy such as: single premium, universal life, universal variable life, the so-called vanishing premium, and the endowment policy.

Single-Premium Policies

Single-premium policies consist of one large, single premium, investment weighted vehicle in which the earnings, if retained until the insured's death, escape inheritance taxes. There may be adverse tax consequences, however, if it takes longer than seven years for the policy to be paid in full. This policy is suitable for people in high-income brackets who can afford a large, single premium, and wish to pass the earnings on the premium income tax-free to their heirs. The earnings may, however, be withdrawn after a designated period of time as a loan at a fixed rate written in the policy.

Universal Life Policies

Universal life policies are a combination of term and whole life insurance. They have a somewhat higher cost and are usually for younger professionals who want the flexibility to vary the premium and face value because of changing incomes and needs. Premiums (minus expense charges) are usually credited to the policyholder's account, from which mortality charges are deducted and interest income is added. The rate of interest being earned on the adjusted savings in the account is usually guaranteed for one year.

Variable Policies

Variable policies are also usually purchased by younger professionals. The main difference between a standard cash-value policy and a variable one is that the investment risk is now borne by the policyholder. The policy offers a split account with term and cash-value components, a fixed premium, and with the investment part directed by the policy owner. The cash value can vary depending on the success of the investment.

Vanishing Premium Policy

The so-called vanishing premium policy simply means that the purchaser front loads the premiums in the early years; then counts on the investment part to do well and to stop paying premiums beyond a certain date (not guaranteed by contract). An advantage is that cash value builds up quickly in the first few years and if investment returns are good, no further premiums are necessary. However, the premiums may not "vanish" if the investment returns are not able to generate enough cash to pay subsequent premiums. The purchaser then has the option of either letting the policy lapse or paying additional premiums later.

Specific Need or Hybrid Policies

These policies are geared for individuals with special needs and include family policies, first-to-die, second-to-die, or adjustable life policies.

Second-to-Die Policies

Second-to-die policies are designed to pay estate taxes upon the death of the surviving spouse. These are cash-value policies that are less expensive because they only pay after the second spouse's death. However, they do not provide any liquidity upon the first spouse's demise and do not offer as much flexibility compared to other insurance products. These policies are often placed in irrevocable trusts, which are designed to minimize federal taxes. Financial advisors can estimate, depending on the tax laws at the current time, the amount of estate tax that will be required upon both spouse's deaths, and therefore suggest the approximate death benefit necessary. Federal estate tax rates are currently much higher than regular income tax rates.

Taxes on estates are calculated based upon the federal unified transfer tax. This transfer tax is composed of the estate tax, the gift tax, and the generation-skipping transfer. What is important is the sum of the assets in the gross estate at death and the total value of taxable gifts made during life. The estate-tax exemption is $2 million for the years 2006–2008 and $3.5 million in 2009. Following those years, the estate tax will be zero in 2010, only to reappear in 2011 unless Congress acts. This means that currently, unless the combined total of all assets in an estate, plus all the lifetime taxable gifts, exceeds $2 million, no estate taxes are imposed. If the amount exceeds $2 million, the lowest effective tax rate is about 37 percent.

Return-of-Premium Policy

A return-of-premium policy is a hybrid product: If the insured dies prior to the term date, beneficiaries receive the face value of the policy. But if the insured lives beyond the term date, all premiums are returned without interest.[3] Compared to the usual level-term policy, the premium is somewhat higher, although not as high as a whole life policy. However, there is a reasonable return on the difference between a level-term policy and the higher return-of-premium policy in the form of return of premiums. The return-of-premium policy is obviously best suited for the healthy, young provider who is betting on outliving the term of the policy. One can get out of a return-of-premium policy and still receive a small fraction of the premiums paid. The other question about a return-of-premium policy that is not yet determined is the tax status of the premium returned at the end of the policy period. The insurance companies argue that the insureds are receiving back the money that was paid in premiums. Prominent sellers of return-of-premium policies include AIG, American General, Genworth, and Lincoln National.

Amount of Life Insurance Needed

Opdyke has summarized the three common methods of determining the amount of life insurance needed.[4,5]

Detailed Analysis of Actual Financial Needs

This method (Figure 6.1) of calculating the amount of insurance needed involves a methodical approach of adding up current living expenses, debts, mortgage payments, retirement requirements for the spouse, emergency cash reserves, children's tuition needs, and any individual needs. On the other side of the ledger, all cash/invested savings, along with educational accounts, are added to come up with approximate future needs—and hence the gap that indicates insurance needs.

Figure 6.1   Example of Determination of Life Insurance Needs

Immediate Cash Needs ($)		Assets ($)		
Death	25,000	Savings/investments liquidated		500,000
Funeral	15,000	Retirement savings		750,000
Medical	25,000	IRA		25,000
Probate fees	5,000	401(k)		25,000
Legal	10,000	Annuities		0
Accounting	3,000	Other		0
Mortgage pay off	250,000	Taxes on lump sum, IRA		0
Other debts			**Sub-Total**	$1,300,000
Loans	0	Other assets		50,000
Car payment	15,000	Rentals		0
Credit card	5,000	Inheritance		0
Living expenses	30,000	Current life insurance		1,000,000
Lost income	100,000	Business ownership		25,000
Home	10,000		**Total**	$2,375,000
Auto	5,000			
Education fund	200,000	Immediate cash needs, total		$3,698,000
Income replacement	3,000,000	Less total assets		−2,375,000
Total	$3,698,000	Life insurance needs		**$1,323,000**

Inflation not factored.

NOTE: This figure appears as Appendix C on the CD so that you can use it as a template.

Income-Replacement Analysis

This method essentially requires an estimate of either the entire income or part of the salary currently earned, and calculating the time period over which it will be needed. For example, if the annual salary is $100,000 and it is estimated that the family will need that income for the next 20 years, then the amount of insurance needed is $2 million. This assumes little cash savings and does not consider inflation or other special factors.

Rule-of-Thumb Method

This very common and simple method estimates life insurance needs based on a multiple of 5 times to 10 times the current annual after-tax income. If the annual after-tax income is $100,000, then a policy of $500,000 to $1 million is recommended. This calculation does not take into consideration inflation, educational needs for children, special needs or any cash reserves.

Income Tax Consequences of Life Insurance

Premiums paid by the policy owner are not currently deductible for federal or state income-tax purposes.

Life insurance proceeds paid by the company at the death of the insured are not included in taxable income for federal and state income-tax purposes. If no beneficiary is indicated, and proceeds end up in the insured's estate, the amount may be subject to federal and state estate and inheritance tax. If a policy is purchased by the physician's corporation, one must be careful to name the corporation as the beneficiary because death benefits payable to someone else (such as a spouse) will be fully taxable upon death.

In general, any cash-value increases within the life insurance policy are not subject to income taxes, and therefore represent a tax shelter of sorts. Expert advice is necessary because specific events may trigger taxes upon withdrawal of cash from the insurance account.

Annuities

Annuities are the exact opposite of traditional insurance. Instead of making regular periodic payments with a goal of a single-death benefit or cash value, a single or several sums are paid to the insurance company in order to receive a series of payments over a period of time. Basically, the insurance company invests the amount paid into the account and makes a profit by keeping the difference between what it pays out in periodic payments and what it earns on either a lump sum or installment payments. If life insurance is seen as protection for the survivors against loss of the insured's income, annuities are purchased to ensure that the insureds do not outlive their savings and other sources of income. As with some insurance products, annuities can also be part of retirement and financial planning and take advantage of tax deferrals.

The various types of annuitization options include: immediate, fixed, variable, and deferred annuities.

Immediate. An immediate annuity involves immediate commencement of payments following a lump-sum payment.

Fixed. With a fixed annuity the purchaser pays a lump sum in return for regular fixed payments to a certain age. The lump sum to be paid is determined by the insurance company. It is based, among other things, on the age at which payments commence.

Variable. A variable annuity is similar to a fixed annuity, except the lump sum is invested by the insurance company in securities whose performance varies. The risk is more or less borne by the annuitant or purchaser.

Deferred. A deferred annuity is often chosen to plan a steady future income stream. In return for either a lump sum or periodic payments, the insurance company promises to pay regular payments to the purchaser sometime in the future.

Important Questions to Answer Before Purchasing a Policy

Buying life insurance is similar to purchasing a car. It can be intimidating and confusing. Insurance comes in all sizes and colors, is essential, one size does not fit all, and buyers should beware. Consider these questions:

- Do I need the insurance and if so, what kind and how much?

- How long does my family need the income replacement if something happened to me?

- What are the tax consequences?

- How does it affect the overall estate plan?

- Am I naming the proper beneficiary?

- Is the price the best I can get?

- What is the insurance company's rating (A.M. Best or Moody's with A+ or AA+ rating)?

- If I switch to a new policy, are the terms the same?

- Does the policy have guaranteed renewability without a physical examination?

- If a term policy, can this be converted to a cash-value policy? What are the conditions?

Tips on Selecting Life Insurance Policies

Following are a few other things to consider when selecting life insurance policies.

Do not falsify the application. Insurance companies use databases such as the Medical Insurance Bureau (MIB)[6] that contain more information about you than you may realize. The MIB is a clearinghouse of medical information on all persons who have applied for life insurance. When an application is filled out, the insurer receives permission to obtain information from the applicant's physicians. If an application is rejected on the basis of false health information, MIB records will reflect the misinformation or lack of honesty. Companies that issue homeowner's and automobile insurance use two common databases, CLUE and A-PLUS,[7,8] to track consumer credit ratings and claim information. The Comprehensive Loss Underwriting Exchange (CLUE) is a database of claims maintained by the firm ChoicePoint that companies query before underwriting or rating policies. The other large database is maintained by the Automobile Property Loss Underwriting Service (A-PLUS), which records property claims by more than 90 percent of insurance companies.

Like other industries, applying for a policy at the end of the quarter or year makes sense because the agent or company probably has quotas they are trying to meet.

If you need a physical examination and must fast, try to get it done early in the morning and prior to any heavy exercise. Stop taking any unnecessary anti-platelet agents, large doses of Tylenol or ibuprofen, and avoid consuming heavy sugar loads.

If rates are decreasing significantly, there is no harm in trying to get a quote on a new policy. Care should be exercised before switching from an older policy to a newer policy. Ask questions about the objective, true cost, and commissions generated for the agent.

Get quotes from at least two agents and use reputable Internet sites to get an idea of price ranges. If premiums sound too good to be true, they probably are.

Check the ratings on insurance companies at sites such as A.R. Best or Moody's. Best's Financial Strength Ratings represent the company's assessment of an insurer's ability to meet its obligations to policyholders based on a proprietary formula, which takes into account the company's performance and comparison to its peers. The ratings scale includes six secure ratings: A++/A+ (superior); A/A– (excellent); B++/B+ (very good); B/B– (fair); C++/C+ (marginal); C/C– (weak); E (under regulatory supervision); F (in liquidation); and S (suspended).

References

1. J. Speer, "Term Life Insurance Prices Drop by Half," National Public Radio, Morning Edition, Nov. 30, 2006, http://www.npr.org/templates/story/story.php?storyId=6559190 (accessed April 30, 2007).

2. K. Spors, "Term-Life Rates Offer Savings for Older People," *Wall Street J*, April 18 (2006): D2.

3. L. Winner, "Getting a Payback," Oct. 25, 2004, USNews.com, www.usnews.com/usnews/biztech/articles/041025/25insurance.htm (accessed June 27, 2006).

4. J.D. Opdyke, "Determining How Much Life Insurance You Need," *Wall Street J*, April 12 (2006): D3.

5. J.D. Opdyke, *The Wall Street Journal Complete Personal Finance Guide Book*, New York: Three Rivers Press (2006).

6. MIB Group Inc., "About MIB," www.mib.com (accessed Oct. 16, 2006).

7. Washington State Office of the Insurance Commissioner, "CLUE (Comprehensive Loss Underwriting Exchange) Fact Sheet," December 2003, www.insurance.wa.gov/factsheets/factsheet_detail.asp?Fct-ShtRcdNum=13 (accessed June 11, 2006).

8. ISO.com, "A-Plus: The Automobile-Property Loss Underwriting Service," www.iso.com/products/2500/prod2551.html (accessed June 11, 2006).

Additional Resources

Accuquote.com provides insurance learning and shopping resources—www.accuquote.com.

A.M. Best provides ratings and analysis of insurance companies—www.ambest.com.

Insure.com is a source of quotes, calculators, legal perspectives, and consumer-oriented advice about all types of insurance—www.insure.com.

Moody's Inc. rates credit worthiness of publicly held companies—www.moodys.com.

The National Insurance Commissioners Organization tracks consumer complaints by state and by trend. It also provides financial profiles and useful information about of insurance companies—www.naic.org.

Chapter 7

Estate Planning Essentials: Protecting Your Family and Your Legacy

Scot C. Crow, JD, LLM, CFP

Estate planning is certainly not something that most people look forward to completing. However, it is necessary to make sure that everything you have worked long and hard to obtain ends up passing to the individuals and charities of your choosing after your death. While there are many details that you will need to learn about regarding trusts, estate taxes, and probate, the following discussion explains some of the estate planning essentials that you should make a priority.

Using the Will to Direct Assets

A will generally spells out what you would like to have done with your assets upon your death. There are several important reasons for preparing a will. You can use a will to:

- Appoint guardians for minor children;

- Appoint an executor and successor executor;

- Provide for property distribution;

- Provide for a trust or life estate (a living trust as an alternative);

- Plan for the payment of debts;

- Provide for the allocation of estate taxes; and

- Provide clauses to reduce the risk of will contests (arguments among the beneficiaries).

If no will is found, the courts will appoint an administrator to administer the estate and distribute property according to state law. If you die without a will (known as dying *intestate*) in most states, your assets will be divided among your immediate family. For example, in Ohio, if you have no children or grandchildren, your estate will go to your spouse. If you have a spouse and one child, your spouse gets the first $20,000, plus one-half of the balance of your estate. The remainder will go to your child. If you have a spouse and more than one child, your spouse gets the first $60,000 or $20,000 depending on whether your spouse is the natural or adoptive parent of one or none of the children. If you do not have a spouse, your children will receive your estate. If you do not have a spouse or children, your parents will receive your estate. If you do not have a spouse, children, or parents, your brothers and sisters will receive your estate.

For a will to be valid, the testator (person making the will) must be over 18 years of age. The will must be in writing and signed at the end by the testator in the presence of at least two competent witnesses. They must not be beneficiaries under the will and must also sign in the presence of each other.

Altering a Will

Testators may change or revoke their wills as often as they desire unless they become insane or of unsound mind, or are under undue influence. The will may be rewritten, or an amendment called a *codicil* may be attached at the end of a will. If a codicil is used, it must be executed with the same formalities as the will. The witnesses do not have to be the same persons who witnessed the previously drawn will. Every will should state at the outset that it is the last will of the testator. Never mark up a will as it may invalidate it.

Surviving-Spouse Protection

In several states, the law provides for certain protections for a surviving spouse. If the will leaves the surviving spouse less than the share of the property to which the surviving spouse would have been entitled had there been no will, he/she has the privilege of choosing whether to accept the will's provisions or to take the share allotted by state law.

It is recommended that every person have a will, even if you think you have all property owned in non-probate form. Something may have been missed, or there could be claims by the estate, such as accidental death, which necessitates a probate process. You should contact your attorney for additional information and assistance in preparing a will.

Living Trusts   If your combined estate, including insurance (group term and individually owned insurance) and retirement plans, is greater than $2 million, you have a federal estate tax problem. However, you may consider implementing a basic family plan now and create an A-B trust plan (described in the following section) in several years or after estate tax reform is more certain.

A family plan presumes that the surviving spouse will inherit all of the deceased spouse's assets. On the death of the survivor, assets will be administered in trust for the benefit of your children. You will not save any estate taxes with a family plan, and by leaving all assets to the surviving spouse, you are not guaranteed that assets will ultimately pass to your descendants.

A relatively common contingent trust for children provides that the assets will be administered as a single fund until the youngest of your children reaches age 21. During that time, the trustee will have sole discretion to pay income and/or principal to your children for their health, education, maintenance, and support. The trustee will also have the power to make advances to children to start a business, get married, or purchase a home. When the youngest child reaches age 21, the trust will be divided into equal shares for each child taking into account any advances. Each child will be entitled to all of the income from his/her share and principal in the trustee's discretion for health, education, maintenance, and support. At certain ages or upon certain events, each child should also have the right to withdraw portions of his/her share.

There are several benefits to creating a family plan. First, it allows you to bifurcate the guardianship role for your children. The guardian of the person for your children may be a wonderful caregiver, but not so wonderful with asset management. With a trust, you can name another person to handle the financial affairs for your children. It is also a way to establish a check-and-balance system between the caregiver and the financial manager.

In addition, if you were to pass assets directly to a minor, those assets would be held by the guardian of the minor on behalf of the minor until age 18. Most clients are not excited about passing significant assets to a child on his or her 18th birthday. A trust allows you to delay distributions, if you wish. Furthermore, the guardian who is entrusted with assets of a minor is subject to the supervision of the probate court. In other words, the guardian must report to the probate court all expenses, investments, and so forth, made on behalf of the minor and is subject to the court's oversight. By transferring assets to a trust for the minor instead of passing them directly to the minor, you can determine the oversight authority (for example, the trustee) and eliminate probate-court filing requirements.

Tax Planning with an A-B Trust

An A-B trust plan is the starting point for any estate tax plan. Unlike the basic family plan, which must be replaced if you wish to do any estate tax planning, you merely build upon an A-B trust plan.

Such a trust provides that upon the first death, the surviving spouse does not inherit directly; rather, the first $2 million of the deceased spouse's assets pass to a Trust B or a credit shelter trust. These assets are not subject to federal tax in the first estate because of the $2-million exemption equivalent, and are not subject to federal tax in the second estate because the spouse did not own the property. If the surviving spouse inherited all of the property directly, it would all be subject to federal estate tax in the survivor's estate, with the benefit of only one $2 million exemption.

The surviving spouse may be the only beneficiary of Trust B (Trust A is the marital share, funded only if the deceased spouse's estate exceeds $2 million). The most that can be given to the surviving spouse without causing Trust B assets to be included in the survivor's estate is:

- All income;
- The right to receive principal for health, maintenance, and support in the accustomed manner of living;
- The right to withdraw for any reason the greater of 5 percent of Trust B or $5,000 (although generally deleting this provision for income-tax reasons is recommended);
- The right to be the trustee;
- The right to appoint property at the survivor's death unequally to children and grandchildren; and
- The right to approve all investments (if not acting as trustee).

Trust A will be taxed in the surviving spouse's estate. The three ways to structure Trust A are:

1. The surviving spouse may have the right to withdraw all assets;

2. Assets may be administered in trust for the survivor's lifetime with the survivor receiving all income and discretionary principal, and having the right to appoint the assets to descendants on death; or

3. Assets may be administered in trust for the survivor's lifetime with the survivor: receiving all income and discretionary principal; having the right to withdraw all of the assets at any time; and having the right to appoint the assets to anyone on death.

Option 2 ensures that assets the surviving spouse does not use will pass to your descendants.

An A-B Trust plan is also a living trust plan. Specifically, you can transfer assets to your A-B Trust during your lifetime to: make the estate administration more efficient upon your death; avoid multiple probate administrations if you have real estate in more than one state; and promote privacy on your death by not having to list assets on a probate inventory. There is no estate tax benefit to funding your trust during your lifetime, but it can make the estate administration process more streamlined.

There are five basic current federal estate tax rules that you should be aware of:

- Each individual currently has a $2-million exemption from the federal estate tax. The exemption is scheduled to increase to $3.5 million by 2009 (see Table 7.1);

- A person may give during life, or leave at death, property to his/her spouse free of estate tax. (The U.S. government waits until the death of the survivor if the assets are left to the surviving spouse);

- After the $2-million exemption, federal estate tax rates start at 37 percent and increase to 47 percent. The top federal estate tax rate will decrease slowly over the next four years;

- Retirement plan assets are subject to both estate tax and income tax; and

Table 7.1   Estate Tax Exemption (July 2006)

Year	Exempted Amount	Estate Tax Rate (%) (Remainder Taxed Up To)
2006	$2 million	46
2007	$2 million	45
2008	$2 million	45
2009	$3.5 million	45
2010	No estate tax	0
2011	$1 million (return to prior tax system as adjusted for inflation)	55
Bill passed by House, held up in the U.S. Senate (June 2006)	$5 million	Tax $20 million at 15% (capital gains rate), tax rate 30% for estates above $25 million
		Thresholds indexed for inflation

- Insurance proceeds for policies owned by a decedent (including group term insurance) are subject to federal estate tax.

Thus, if one spouse leaves all of his/her assets to the other, there would be no federal estate tax due at the first death, but only one $2-million exemption would be available. The use of an A-B Trust makes it possible to leave assets to a spouse and get the benefit of two exemptions—a savings of significant federal estate taxes.

To ensure maximum estate tax savings from an A-B Trust plan, it is important that assets are transferred to a spouse's trust during lifetime or at death (via the will or beneficiary designations). If, for example, on the death of one spouse, all assets pass to a surviving spouse, the deceased spouse's estate tax credit will not be maximized (that is, Trust B will not be fully funded). It is important to review the title of assets and beneficiary designations to maximize the potential of the A-B Trust plan.

Financial Power of Attorney

A financial power of attorney is a document whereby you, known as the *principal*, appoint another individual, known as the *attorney-in-fact*, to make financial and business decisions on your behalf.

The power of attorney can be limited, giving the attorney-in-fact only very limited powers (such as the power to transfer the principal's assets to a trust established by the principal), or it can be general, giving the attorney-in-fact all of the powers that the principal would have if personally present. Further, the document can be prepared so that the powers begin as soon as the document is signed and continue indefinitely or for a restricted time period. It can also be prepared so that the powers come into effect in the future when a particular event occurs (for example, when you are no longer competent—perhaps due to a physical or mental illness).

The most common power of attorney estate planners prepare is that of a durable nature. What makes a power of attorney durable is the language in the document providing that the power of attorney will remain in effect even if the principal becomes incapacitated. Thus, if the principal becomes incapacitated for a short or long period of time, someone will have the power and authority to act on the principal's behalf. This can be a very broad, all-inclusive power, or it may be limited to certain business affairs. This document may be broadened to designate who you would like to serve as your guardian or the guardian of your minor child or children, if one were required.

Living Wills and Other Health Care Planning Documents

A living will is generally a state-prescribed form in which you place in writing your wishes about life-sustaining treatments should you become permanently unconscious or terminally ill and unable to communicate. Some important things to remember about a living will are that it:

- Allows you to establish in advance the type of medical care you would want to receive if you were to become terminally ill, and to tell your physician or family what kind of life-sustaining treatments you want to receive;

- Is used only in limited situations when you are unable to tell your physician what kind of health care services you want to receive. For example, in Ohio, before a living will would go into effect, you must be either terminally ill (two physicians have determined that you have no reasonable chance of recovery), and unable to tell your physician your wishes regarding health care services; or permanently unconscious (two physicians—one of whom must be a medical specialist in an appropriate field—decide that you have no reasonable possibility of regaining consciousness); and

- May give the physician the authority to withhold all life-sustaining treatment and permit you to die naturally and take no action to postpone your death, providing you with only that care necessary to make you comfortable and relieve pain. This may include writing a do-not-resuscitate (DNR) order, withdrawing life-sustaining treatment such as CPR, or removing nutrition and hydration, but only if you have expressed that desire on the form.

Health Care Power of Attorney

A health care power of attorney is a state-prescribed form that allows you to appoint someone (an attorney-in-fact) to make medical decisions for you in the event that you are unable to do so. It differs from the living will because the attorney-in-fact appointed is authorized to make medical decisions in any situation when the patient is unable to communicate. It is not limited to the event of becoming permanently unconscious or terminally ill and unable to communicate.

There are two important things to remember about a health care power of attorney. First, you may name a person to act on your behalf to make health care decisions for you, if you become unable to make them for yourself. Second, the person appointed as the attorney-in-fact has the power to authorize and refuse medical treatment. This authority is recognized in all medical situations when you are unable to express your own wishes.

Table 7.2   Comparison of Trusts

Type of Trust	Reason for Trust	Asset Value
Revocable living trust	Ensure privacy; avoid probate; management of assets in the event of death or disability	No minimum
Qualified terminal interest property	Avoid tax on death of first spouse and provide for distribution of trust assets after spouse's death	No minimum
Asset protection	Protect beneficiary's assets from creditors	No minimum
Special-needs trust	Provide assets for disabled child without disqualifying said child from state funding programs	No minimum
Irrevocable-insurance trust	Avoid estate tax on insurance proceeds	No minimum
Marital-bypass trust	Utilize estate tax exemption for both spouses	>$2 million exemption
Charitable-remainder trust	Eliminates taxes on the sale of a capital asset and creates income tax deduction for donors	No minimum
Grantor-retained annuity trust	Freeze the value of assets and transfer assets free of gift and estate taxes	No minimum
Charitable-lead annuity trust	Reduce estate taxes and pass assets to heirs and charity	No minimum

Source: K. Hube, "Just Like Bill Gates," *Wall Street Journal*, June 26, 2006, R4-5.

Do-Not-Resuscitate Comfort Care Program

Some states offer a DNR comfort care program as an advance directive that allows you the option of not being resuscitated in the event of a cardiac or respiratory arrest. By enrolling in this program, you have a choice to die without heroic measures, and health care providers are provided with legal means to respect those wishes.

Conclusion

A cursory review of the types of trusts available (see Table 7.2) should be supplemented by legal advice. Also, an assessment of one's financial goals, current financial position, and values are all highly advised. All estate planning documents can be prepared by the same attorney as a package. Frequent changes in federal and state laws require updating these documents at least every three or four years, and sooner if a change in personal circumstances occurs.

Chapter 8

Disability Insurance: Protect Your Income When Illness or Injury Occurs

Physicians, like other professionals, tend to underestimate the need for a disability insurance policy and concentrate on other insurance needs (health, life, auto, and home). According to the National Council on Disability, the number of Americans who are disabled has grown to 54 million and the number of employers offering long-term disability coverage is down to 40 percent.[1] The Society of Actuaries states that the chance of a long-term disability (more than 90 days) is likely to affect a third of all adults compared to the chance of death (one in seven) in adults less than 65 years in age.

Only 13 percent of disabilities are due to injury.[2] Once a physician has an illness, the odds of being able to get a long-term disability policy that is affordable is slim. The definition of disability has changed significantly because of losses suffered by insurance carriers.

Disability

Common Causes of Disability

There are many causes of disability, including:

- Back problems: 18.2 percent;
- Emotional/psychiatric problems: 12.7 percent;
- Neurologic: 11.3 percent;
- Extremities: 9 percent; and
- Cardiovascular: 4.1 percent.[3]

Types of Coverage

Disability coverage comes in two forms. One is the individual policy. Premiums can be paid by the physician or the corporation. If the corporation pays the premium, the benefits are taxable. If the individual pays the premiums, the benefits are tax-free. The other is a group disability policy. Part or all of the premiums are paid by the employer and are a legitimate business expense. Even if the employer does not pay the entire premium, rates are generally cheaper when purchased through large entities (universities/chambers of commerce).

Total vs. Residual Disability

A typical definition of *own occupation total disability* includes the inability to perform the material and substantial duties of the applicant's regular occupation (the occupation you are engaged in at the time of disability). Under this coverage, the insurer will pay the claim for disability even if the applicant is working in some other capacity different than your *own* occupation. Most insurance companies have stopped offering own occupation policies and instead are offering replacement income policies. These policies may contain language that reads: "Because of sickness or injury you are unable to perform the material and substantial duties of your occupation and are not engaged in any other occupation." Physicians must carefully read the contract, particularly the exact wording that defines a disability. Language that reads: "Because of sickness or injury you are unable to perform the material and substantial duties of your occupation or any occupation for which you are deemed reasonably qualified by education, training or experience" leaves the decision regarding the kind of work the physician is qualified for up to the insurance carrier.

Residual disability means that the physician is still capable of performing substantial work, but suffers either a loss of income (more than 20 percent) or loss of time and duties as a result of the disability. Most disability claims start out or end as residual disability claims.

Insurance Coverage and Payments for Claims

To calculate how much disability coverage is appropriate, start with a general idea of how much income will be needed to live on, assuming that expenses will have to be cut. No insurance company will cover 100 percent of predisability income. Payments by insurers are based on loss of income. For residual disability, most will cover in the range of 60 percent of pretax income and most important, in most cases the physician has to show a loss of at least 20 percent of predisability income for the policy to take effect. As an example, if your monthly income is $15,000 per month and your post-disability income is $5,000 per month, the loss of income is $10,000. Clearly, you have lost more than 20 percent of your base income. The insurance policy generally pays benefits in proportion to the loss of earnings.

Most policies also have caps on how much per month will be paid in case of partial (residual) or total disability. Because insurers do not want incentives for physicians to not work, the higher the ceiling, the higher the premium will be.

CAUTION: A contract for disability insurance may contain 25 or more pages. While it may seem a bother to read such a long document, be aware that certain clauses or definitions in contracts may later become major issues when you try to collect on the policy. For example, some contracts use these two definitions:

- *Current monthly earnings* means the monthly earnings you receive from any employer or for any work while disabled under this plan; and

- *Average monthly pay* means the monthly average of earnings, bonuses, and commissions paid to you over the pay period shown on your certificate validation form (referring to income from your employer only).

Because the employer pays for most group disability policies, the insurance company regards the average predisability monthly pay as only the pay you receive from that employer with whom they have a contract. But, like many physicians, you may obtain additional income from a consulting or part-time job, such as reading tests/electrocardiograms at home for a private company. In this case, the insurance company will calculate the average monthly pay (before your disability) as the earnings from your employer, but will include all earned income (from sources other than your employer).

Let us assume you are paid $100,000 per year from your employer (or practice corporation) and you have outside earned income from other sources for professional services of $40,000 annually. Following disability, your income from your employer for part-time work is now paying $50,000 annually, and you maintain your outside income for a total earned income of $90,000. The insurer may contend that while your average monthly income for purposes of calculating premiums and insuring you against disability was $8,333 ($100,000 divided by 12), you are actually earning $7,500 a month ($90,000 divided by 12) and have not lost more than 20 percent of your total earned income (20 percent of $90,000 equals $18,000). This language is a common trap that physicians are unaware of when reading through a standard contract. Physicians should ask the insurance agent to send them a statement that will either include all earned income (from the employer as well as other sources) as "average monthly income" or exclude outside earned income from "current monthly earnings." If a physician does not have any outside income and is not likely to, then the clause is not an issue.

Taxation of Disability Income

Any disability income from an individual policy is tax free when the premiums were paid with after-tax dollars by the physician. Because employers pay all or part of the premium on group disability policies, any income is taxable. If a percentage of the premium was paid by the physician, then that proportion is not taxable.

Short-Term vs. Long-Term Coverage

Less than half of disability claimants younger than 40 years of age continue to receive disability payments 5 years later.[2] Some employers provide short-term disability coverage (less than 90 days), and have group policies that provide long-term coverage after 90 days of an illness or disability. This is because the longer the "elimination period" before the insurer starts paying, the less expensive the policy is. Physicians with enough savings built up may be better off with a longer elimination period of 180 days.

Questions and Answers About Disability Insurance

How Long Will the Disability Payments Continue?

In general, most insurance companies now only cover disability until age 65. The shorter the benefit period, the cheaper the premiums are. Policies that provide coverage until death are fairly expensive.

Can I Get Additional Disability Insurance (Future Options)?

An optional rider can be purchased at the time of first becoming insured to ensure enough coverage as income goes up. The insurance company usually provides the physician several opportunities to purchase additional insurance over time with proof of increased earnings (a tax return). The advantage is that the benefit is increased without any additional evidence of insurability (health status).

What About Cost-of-Living Adjustments?

A cost-of-living adjustment (COLA) is an important feature of disability policies and adds cost to the premium. A COLA rider to the policy is effective only when a physician files a disability claim, and usually if the disability lasts longer than 12 months. The rider is meant to be a hedge against inflation and increases the monthly benefit every year while you are disabled. The percentage annual adjustment to the basic disability benefit is usually tied to a benchmark such as the consumer price index or the interest rate of a U.S. Treasury bill.

Will the Disability Insurance Cover the Inability to Practice a Medical Sub-Specialty?

Older policies were issued by insurers that covered physicians for their "own occupation." Increasingly, premiums are significantly greater for coverage of "own occupation" instead of "any occupation." The latter means that if you are a neurologist and can work as a primary care physician, the benefits will stop.

Can the Insurance Company Cancel My Policy?

A non-cancelable and renewable feature adds to the cost of the policy, but for most physicians this is a valuable feature worth paying for. A lesser form of coverage is simply a guaranteed renewable feature. The latter implies that the insurance carrier will probably not change anything about the policy. However, that does not mean they cannot change the premium in a given year for a particular occupation or a class of people (not an individual) with approval from the state. The "Cadillac" feature is the non-cancelable and renewable. A non-cancelable policy means that the insurance company guarantees fixed benefits for a fixed premium.

What Is the Waiver of Premium Feature?

This rider on your disability policy means that while you are determined to have total or residual disability, all premiums are waived.

Can I Obtain Multiple Policies from Different Carriers to Increase My Coverage?

At the time of an application, the physician will be required to disclose other disability policies that have been purchased. Although there may not be any legal restrictions on the number of separate policies or amount of coverage, most insurance companies will restrict the amount of coverage offered if the total benefit exceeds the current income.

When Disabled, What Is the Procedure to Obtain Lost Income from the Insurer?

As soon as you have an operation or illness that will entail time off, a letter should be sent to the insurance company informing them of the illness, the date it began, and the likely time period you will be disabled. You will be sent forms to fill out asking for details and your treating physician's report. If the policy kicks in after 90 days, more forms are sent to ascertain average monthly income prior to the disability and current monthly earnings after the disability. This allows the company to calculate your exact loss of income. A check will be mailed to you based on this information.

Every month that you are disabled, standard forms will be sent for you to fill out, including a detail of your daily schedule of work. A more detailed report is required at the end of the year. The company often sends its representative at the end of the year to interview you in your work surroundings to confirm your disability.

A questionnaire is often sent (with your permission) to the hospital where you work seeking documentation of your activity level and a list of procedures you performed. Your accountant is contacted for information on your income from various other sources. Tax returns are usually requested by the insurance company within the first year for confirmation of earned income. Investment income or dividends and income from non-professional sources are not taken into account for calculating benefits. If there is something unusual or conflicting information is provided, the insurance company may investigate and confirm your activity and disability level.

Can I Engage in Other Occupations and Have the Income Not Be Counted Toward My Current Monthly Income?

If your other business or work is not related to your occupation, the income will not count to calculate your current monthly income. It is best to notify the insurance company describing the exact nature of the work (using terms such as *consulting*, *legal review*, and so forth) before starting the work. In general, deferred compensation (i.e., retirement plans) is not considered as current monthly income for calculation of your monthly benefit. If you are receiving any other benefits such as from a workers' compensation fund or Social Security Disability Insurance, you are required to indicate the amounts on the form mailed to the insurance company as it may affect the payments to you.

What If the Disability Is Residual and Is Likely To Persist Until Age 65? What Options Are There?

Residual disability (as opposed to permanent disability) is when the physician is not able to practice his/her occupation, and has a significant reduction in income (as mentioned before, usually a reduction of more than 20 percent). If the policy pays until age 65, one option is to continue sending in monthly forms, including income for the month and a physician's statement stating continuing disability. In some cases, the insurance company will allow the treating physician to send the disability statement once every three or four months. This can continue for the life of the policy.

Another option, often proposed by the insurance company in cases where the residual disability is likely to continue and possibly worsen, is to pay the physician a lump sum and terminate the policy. The insurance company is able to avoid the future risk of paying even more if the disability worsens; decrease overhead by cutting back the paperwork; and improve its balance sheet by taking future losses off the books. For the physician the advantages are no paperwork; no unnecessary visits to the treating physician; the ability to invest the lump sum (received tax-free in an individual policy) where he/she wants; and having dollars in hand to leave for heirs. If the physician dies before the term of the policy (barring any provisions in the policy), the heirs do not receive any further payments. The amount of the lump sum is based on calculating the net present value of all future payments likely to be paid until age 65 by deciding on a certain discount rate.

What Are Exclusion Clauses I Should Know About?

There are several exclusions to keep in mind, including:

- Mental health exclusion: Some policies have a two-year benefit period if disability is caused by depression, dementia, stress disorder, or anxiety;

- Drug or alcohol exclusion: Many policies have a one-year maximum benefit period for drugs or alcohol;

- Exclusion for disability during commitment of a crime; and

- Act of war: Exclusion if disability occurs because of an act of war.

How Do I Appeal the Insurance Company's Decision?

If you disagree with a denial decision, the Employee Retirement Income Security Act of 1974 (ERISA) provides you with the right to appeal the decision and review pertinent documents in your claim file. This is a federal law that affects some administrative aspects of employee benefit and retirement plans. If a company offers employees certain benefit plans, such as health insurance or a retirement plan, the company is subject to certain requirements under ERISA.

If you do not agree with the reason why your claim was denied in whole or in part and you wish to appeal the decision, you must write to the company within 60 days of the date of the denial letter. Your letter, which must be signed and dated by you or your legal representative, should clearly outline your position and any issues or comments you have in connection with your claim and the company's decision to deny your request for benefits under the policy. Upon completion of this review, the insurance company will advise you of its further determination.

What Are Signs that the Insurance Company Is Acting in "Bad Faith"?

Concerns about how the claim is handled may occur if the insurance company is:

- Misrepresenting pertinent facts of insurance policy provisions relating to the coverage at issue;

- Failing to acknowledge and act reasonably and promptly on communications with respect to claims arising out of insurance policies;

- Failing to adopt and implement reasonable standards for the prompt investigation of claims arising under insurance policies;

- Refusing to pay claims without conducting a reasonable investigation based upon all available information;

- Failing to confirm or deny coverage of claims within a reasonable time after proof of loss statement has been completed;

- Not attempting in good faith to effectuate fair and equitable settlements of claims in which liability has become reasonably clear;

- Compelling insureds to institute litigation to recover amounts due under an insurance policy by offering substantially less than the amount ultimately recovered in actions brought by such insureds;

- Attempting to settle a claim for less than the amount to which a reasonable person would have believed he/she was entitled by reference to written or printed advertising material accompanying or made part of an application;

- Attempting to settle claims on the basis of an application, which was altered without notice to, or knowledge or consent of the insured; and

- Making claims payments to insured or beneficiaries not accompanied by a statement setting forth the coverage under which the payments are being made.

Where Should I Complain About an Insurance Company?

The best place is usually the insurance commissioner in each state. A copy to the Better Business Bureau should also be sent. Most states have Websites where one can write in a complaint and the insurance company is required to respond within a certain period of time.

Resources

1. D. Mackeen, "The Disability Dilemma," *SmartMoney*, July 2005, 70–75.

2. National Institute on Disability and Rehabilitation Research, *Disability in the United States Prevalence and Causes*. Washington, DC: National Institute on Disability and Rehabilitation Research (1992).

3. Health Insurance Association of America, *Source Book of Health Insurance Data 1999–2000*. Washington, DC: Health Insurance Association of America (2001).

Additional Resources

See or download a sample disability policy from www.toolkit.cch.com/tools/downloads/disablty.rtf.

See Appendix D for a list of state insurance commissioners. You can also go to the National Association of Insurance Commissioners Website at www.naic.org.

Chapter 9

Saving for Higher Education Expenses

Establishing a college savings plan for children is a priority right behind an emergency cash fund, essential insurance policies, and a retirement account. It is intimidating to think about the current cost of college tuition and what direct and indirect college costs might be 15 or 20 years from now. The average annual cost of tuition and fees at 4-year public colleges reached $5,491 in the 2005–2006 academic year, which was up about 7 percent from the previous year.[1] Four-year private college annual costs increased almost 6 percent during the same period to more than $29,000.[1]

Unfortunately, not having a college degree puts the child at a serious disadvantage and is likely to be a handicap throughout adult life. A bachelor's degree, according to the U.S. Census Bureau, is worth almost 62 percent more earning power on average than a high-school diploma and more than $1 million over a lifetime. All parents are aware of the importance of a college degree. However, they are caught between not saving enough so their child is eligible for assistance, and saving to a point at which they will not ask for assistance.

Expected Family Contribution (EFC)

The expected family contribution (EFC) is a crucial piece of information that assists financial aid counselors in determining a student's need for financial assistance in attending college. The EFC is the amount the student's family can be expected to provide toward his/her college tuition and other expenses. This is calculated by the federal government based on the student's and family's income, number of family members, and the number of college students in the family. Financial aid administrators determine an applicant's need for federal student aid from the U.S. Department of Education and other non-federal sources of assistance by subtracting the EFC from the student's cost of attendance (COA).

Getting Started: Using the FAFSA to Apply for Aid

Financial aid administrators use the information from the Free Application for Federal Student Aid (FAFSA), including the EFC, to develop a financial aid package. This aid package specifies the types and amounts of assistance, including non-federal aid that a student will receive to cover his/her education-related expenses up to COA.

A FAFSA application may be submitted directly online (www.fafsaonline.com), through the school, or by mail. Using the electronic format can alert you to any missed sections. There may be a costly delay if a paper application must be retuned to you for correction or additional information via mail.

Finding Financial Aid: Grants, Loans, and Other Sources

According to the College Board, students received over $122 billion in aid for undergraduate and graduate study in 2004.[1] The federal government provided more than $111 billion of the amount (Table 9.1). A school's financial aid office generally determines the programs and amounts of aid an applicant receives. Specific aid programs can be need-based or non–need based. The exact amount of aid offered to an applicant varies primarily according to the applicant's eligibility, the regulatory guidelines, and the resources available to the institution. There are four main categories of financial aid, which are discussed in the following sections:

- Grants and scholarships;

- Loans;

- Personal savings; and

- Work–study programs.

Table 9.1   Financial Aid from All Sources (2003)

Type of Aid	Total Amount of Aid	Percent of Total Aid	Average Award for Undergraduates
Institutional	$23.2 billion	19.0%	$4,257
Federal grants	$17.2 billion	14.0%	$2,609
State aid	$6 billion	5.0%	$2,070
Private scholarship aid (estimated)	$3.1–$3.3 billion	2%–3%	$1,982
Federal Perkins loans	$1 billion	1.0%	$1,948
Total aid (without private scholarships)	$122 billion	98.0%	$7,350
Aid from all sources	$124.5–$125.3 billion		

Adapted from www.ihep.org/Pubs/PDF/privatescholarshipscount.pdf. Used with permission from the Institute for Higher Education.

Grants and Scholarships

These may be awarded for academic merit, athletic ability, artistic talent, a particular field of study, or by far the most common reason, financial need. Grants and scholarships are highly sought after because no repayment of funds is required. The College Board has estimated that the average grant per full-time equivalent student was $3,968 in 2003.[1] Private scholarships from foundations, corporations, research centers, individuals, and other private sources totaled between $3.1 billion and $3.4 billion in 2003–2004, accounting for about 7 percent of grant-based aid and 2–3 percent of all student aid.[2] This indicates that grant or scholarship assistance probably covers about one-third of the total aid provided for college. Merit scholarships were 16 percent ($7.3 billion) of all college financial aid grants in the U.S. for the academic years 2003–2004.[3] The usual sources for help in locating grants or scholarships are school guidance counselors. Various organizations and online databases can be searched for leads as well.

Pell grants come from a need-based grant program for undergraduate students. Most Pell grants are given to those with family incomes less than $20,000. Eligibility is based on federal EFC.

Federal supplemental education opportunity grants are given by another need-based grant program provided to colleges for undergraduate students. The maximum award is $4,000 per year.

Loans

According to data compiled by the College Board, loans for college education have increased by 137 percent over the past decade and are the most common source of funding. Despite the interest on the loan being tax deductible, the problem is the amount of debt a family and the student is under if a loan is the only source of funding. Loans can be private or federal/state, and subsidized or unsubsidized.

Federal loans include those through the Perkins loan program—a subsidized loan with a 5-percent fixed interest rate for undergraduate students and "exceptional" graduate students. The U.S. Department of Education provides the funding to the college. The college determines need, combines the funds with its own to allow flexible repayment terms, and offers numerous deferment options. Repayment is due nine months after a student graduates, withdraws, or attends school less than half time.

Stafford loans are the most common source of college loan funds. They are fixed-rate, low-interest loans (maximum of 6.8 percent as of July 1, 2006) available to undergraduate students attending accredited schools at least half time. Annual limits for borrowing are: $3,500 for freshmen, $4,500 for sophomores, and up to $5,500 for juniors and seniors. Stafford loans are funded by private lenders but guaranteed by the federal government. For subsidized loans, the government pays the interest while a student is in school; for unsubsidized loans, the student is responsible for paying the interest while in school. The cost (in 2006–2007) is up to 3 percent in fees, which includes a 2-percent federal origination fee and a 1-percent federal default fee. Repayment is due six months after the student graduates, withdraws, or attends school less than half time.

Personal Savings

The surest way for helping your child with college is through a disciplined savings account earmarked for college education. The magic of compounding makes it imperative that some sort of tax-advantaged educational savings plan be started very early, even if the amounts are relatively small and the projected target seems far away.

Work–Study Programs

Federal or individual college work–study programs help many students with tuition and living expenses by providing part-time community or on-campus work for students deserving of financial need.

Formulas for Determining Financial Aid

The method for determining federal aid differs from institution to institution because of "institutional methodology" and internal differences relating to grants and scholarships. The assets excluded from the EFC for federal aid, such as primary home equity and certain investments, may be considered as part of EFC by some institutions. In general, the main factor determining aid under federal guidelines has to do with the amount of assets owned by the student and parents.

Student Assets

Two areas are considered when student assets are reviewed:

- 25–35 percent of all student assets (cash, investments, businesses, and real estate, and including those under the Uniform Gifts to Minors Act (UGMA) and the Uniform Transfers to Minors Act (UTMA), are considered available for college expenses. As an example, if a UGMA account has $25,000, the eligibility for financial aid will be reduced by $6,250 to $8,750; and

- 50 percent of a student's income (after some allowances) is considered available.

Parental Assets

Four areas of assets are considered when parental assets are reviewed:

- 0–5.6 percent of parental assets (cash, investments, businesses, and real estate but not retirement accounts) are considered available for assisting the student's college expenses. As an example, assets of $50,000 will decrease eligibility for financial aid by up to $2,800 per year;

- 22–47 percent of a parent's income (based on a sliding-income scale and after certain allowances) is considered available;

- Any equity in a primary home, insurance policies, and annuities are excluded from a calculation of the EFC; and

- All "qualified" retirement accounts, whether owned by the student or the parent, are not included in the EFC for calculating federal financial aid.

Grandparent or Other Relative Assets

Assets of grandparents or other relatives do not count in any financial aid formula. A contribution by a relative may not trigger any federal gift tax for the donor, but may have consequences for the student. If the relative makes a tuition payment directly to the college on behalf of the student, the eligibility for aid will be reduced on a dollar-for-dollar basis. Instead, the student may be better served by a gift to a 529 savings plan set up by the parents. A large amount, up to $60,000 for an individual and $120,000 for a married couple, can be contributed to such a plan with a relatively small effect (a 5.6 percent decrease) on the aid formula. The donors are still liable for a gift tax on more than $24,000 (for a couple). However, the gift can be prorated using the tax exemption over 5 years to avoid the tax. Two sets of grandparents can double that amount. Another option for grandparents or relatives may be to pay off the student's loans after college graduation.

Types of College Savings Plans

According to a recent survey by Fidelity Investments, less than one-quarter of parents saving for college are using 529 plans, while 52 percent use bank savings accounts and 29 percent use U.S. savings bonds.[4,5] Following are the various advantages and disadvantages of these common savings plans (Table 9.2).

Table 9.2   Types of Educational Savings Accounts

	Taxable Account (mutual funds)	U.S. Savings Bonds	Custodial Account (UGMA/UTMA account)	Coverdell Education Savings Account (ESA)	529 State Prepaid Plan	529 College Savings Plan
Purpose and use	Invest in funds for educational or other needs (any purpose)	Invest in conservative, guaranteed bonds for educational or other needs	Invest for a minor for any expense that benefits the child	Invest for any educational level (primary, secondary, or higher education)	Prepay for qualified college tuition and fees, and sometimes room and board	Invest tax-free for qualified college expenses
Controlled by	Owner	Owner	Custodian, until child is of age	Person establishing the account	Person establishing the account	Person establishing the account
Types of investment	Mutual funds	Series I and Series EE U.S. savings bonds	UGMA, mutual funds, stocks, bonds	Assets can be invested in stocks, bonds, mutual funds, and cash equivalents. Investments can be bought and sold as desired.	Tuition units or contracts	Professional asset management. Most plans permit several mutual fund investments. Investment choice may be changed once a year.
Contribution limit	None	Maximum annual purchase is $30,000 ($60,000 per couple) in TreasuryDirect, and paper bonds, each.	No limit. Gift tax for amounts >$12,000 per donor	Up to $2,000 a year	Maximum varies by state, but plans cover, in general, up to five years of college costs	Lifetime maximum of total of about $300,000 for some plans; may pay gift taxes if more than $12,000 a year.
Restrictions on income	None	For tax year 2006, <$78,100 for singles; <$124,700 for joint filers	None	For single filers, $95,000–$110,000; for joint filers, $190,000–$220,000.	None	None

(Table continued on next page)

Table 9.2 Types of Educational Savings Accounts (continued)

	Taxable Account (mutual funds)	U.S. Savings Bonds	Custodial Account (UGMA/UTMA account)	Coverdell Education Savings Account (ESA)	529 State Prepaid Plan	529 College Savings Plan
Federal tax consequences	Up to 15% tax on capital gains and dividend income.	Interest earned is tax-free if used for qualified higher education purposes.	Children's earnings: Over 18: Taxed at child's rate. Under 18: Less than $850 tax-free. Next $850 taxed at child's rate. Excess of $1,700 taxed at parents' highest marginal rate.	Qualified distributions tax-free	Qualified distributions tax-free. (Some states may also offer tax breaks.)	Qualified distributions tax-free. (Some states may also offer tax breaks.)
State tax consequences	Yes	No	Depends on child's age	Varies by state	Varies by state	Varies by state
Penalties for non-qualified withdrawals	No	Three months of interest forfeited if redeemed within first 5 years	No	Federal income tax plus 10% penalty tax	Federal income tax plus 10% penalty tax	Federal income tax plus 10% penalty tax
Effect on federal aid	Considered parent's or other owner's assets	Considered parent's or other owner's assets, depending on the tax bracket	Considered student's assets	Considered parental asset.	Generally considered parent's or other owner's assets	Considered asset of parent or other account owner
Use of funds	No limit	Tuition and mandatory fees	Anything that benefits the minor.	Postsecondary costs; K–12 costs	For most plans, tuition, fees, room and board.	Qualified college expenses
Change beneficiary	Yes	Yes	No	Yes	Yes	Yes
Estate planning consequence	Remain in owner's estate	Bonds remain in owner's estate	Removed from estate	Removed from estate	Contributions not included in estate	Contributions not included in estate

Source: U.S. Securities and Exchange Commission, Internal Revenue Service.

Savings Bonds

Advantages

- Safe investment backed by the U.S. government;

- Distributions from EE bonds purchased after 1989 and all I bonds are tax free, provided income limits are met and funds are used for qualified education expenses;

- There is no penalty if funds are used for other purposes than college; and

- There is no state or local income tax on the interest.

Disadvantages

- The purchaser of the bond has to be 24 years old;

- Three months interest is forfeited if the bond is redeemed before five years;

- There is an income limitation in order to exempt the interest even if the proceeds are used for qualified education expenses. The threshold is more than $76,200 (single) or $121,850 (married filing jointly);

- Only tuition and fees are qualified education expenses; and

- Only the bondholder, his/her spouse, or a dependent can claim the interest exclusion. A grandparent cannot claim the exclusion unless he/she is claiming the grandchild as a dependent.

Coverdell Education Savings Account

The Coverdell education savings account (ESA) is intended to provide funding for qualified educational expenses for your children, grandchildren, or other eligible recipients. ESAs are typically used to complement other college savings plans.

Advantages

- There is a large variety of investment options;

- Earnings are not taxable while in the account;

- Contributions to a ESA can be made on behalf of the same beneficiary for whom the donor makes a contribution to a 529 college savings plan;

- Qualified expenses include tuition, fees, books, room and board, tutoring, supplies, uniforms, transportation, and the purchase of computer technology, or equipment used while attending an eligible educational institution; and

- There is a key difference between a 529 savings plan and a ESA plan. Unlike a 529 plan, the ESA can be used to fund not only college, vocational schools, and universities, but also public, private, or religious K–12 schools.

Disadvantages

- The yearly contribution limit in 2006 is $2,000;

- Eligibility to contribute is determined by adjusted gross income (AGI). The phase-out range for single-tax filers in 2006 is $95,000–$110,000 of AGI and $190,000–$220,000 of AGI for those filing jointly;

- The beneficiary has to be younger than 18 years of age and contributions have to stop at this age;

- If the funds are not used for college, they are the property of your child and cannot be returned back to you unlike the 529 plans; and

- If more money is withdrawn than the "qualified higher education expense," the excess will be subject to taxes and a penalty of 10 percent.

529 College Savings Plan

The 529 plans come in two ways: prepaid tuition plans and college savings plans. All 50 states and the District of Columbia sponsor at least one type of 529 plan. In addition, a group of private colleges and universities sponsor a prepaid tuition plan. These tax-advantaged savings plans, legally known as "qualified tuition plans," are authorized by Section 529 of the Internal Revenue Code.

These 529 college savings plans vary state by state, but in general, permit non-taxable savings for higher education.

Advantages

- Funds can be utilized for any college in the United States;

- Depending on the state of residence, a variety of investments may be available, including mutual funds;

- The savings plan is funded by after-tax contributions, but the distributions for qualified education expenses do not incur any federal tax;

- There may be state income tax benefits for residents, including deductions for the contribution. The 529 plans are considered municipal securities. State tax may be due if withdrawals are made to pay for qualified expenses outside of the sponsor's state;

- If a parent is the donor, financial aid will only count for 5.6 percent in the ECF;

- If a child does not end up going to college, the donor can get the funds back but would owe taxes and a 10-percent penalty on any gains (not the basis);

- Eligibility to contribute is open to parents, grandparents, relatives, siblings, and friends with no income restrictions; and

- Annual contribution limits vary by state. In most states, you can contribute up to $12,000 per year or $24,000 per couple in 2006 without a gift tax. Another option is to contribute $60,000 from an individual (or $120,000 for married couples filing jointly) per beneficiary via a one-shot contribution, but prorate the amount over 5 years. For high-income earners, this also removes assets from your estate.

Disadvantages

- The plan still dictates investment choices and it can only be changed once a year;

- The cost of the plan is somewhat higher compared to the owner managing the funds in a regular account but should total less than 1.5 percent of assets;

- Distributions must be used for qualified higher-education expenses such as tuition, room and board, or else the distribution is treated as ordinary income along with a 10-percent penalty. The penalty may be waived in case of death or disability of the beneficiary, or if the beneficiary receives a scholarship. Although most states allow a change in beneficiary, the change in beneficiary must be to a first cousin or closer to the original beneficiary;

- A disadvantage for donors is that because the donor owns the account, Medicaid may insist that the funds be used if the donor should need nursing home care and not have other funds available; and

- Not all states have protections against a donor's creditors.

Not all 529 college savings plans are the same. The mutual fund investment rating firm Morningstar rated the top plans[6] and determined that for those investing directly rather than through brokers, top-performing funds included: the Alaska T. Rowe Price college savings plans, for those who desire active management of the fund; and the Utah Educational Savings Plan Trust, for those who wish to invest via index funds.

For those who choose to invest through a broker, the Morningstar reviewers highly rated the Virginia CollegeAmerica (American Funds) and the Colorado Scholars Choice.

Section 529 Prepaid Tuition Programs in Depth

Most prepaid programs are state-sponsored and allow parents or anyone else to purchase tuition credits on behalf of a beneficiary. In a state-sponsored program, the maximum benefit is obviously derived by the student going to an in-state college. Unfortunately, most prepaid tuition programs are closed to new investors because the trustees did not sufficiently anticipate inflationary cost of education.

Advantages[7]

- No income restrictions are imposed on donor;

- Benefits are federally tax exempt if used for qualified expenses;

- If the child attends a school within the plan, costs are covered by credits or certificates purchased;

- By buying prepaid tuition credits, you lock in future tuition costs at today's rates;

- There may be state tax breaks when you contribute; and

- No investment risk, unless the state mismanages the funds; and

- Has low fees. The national average for expenses is about 1.4 percent per year for private and up to 5.75 percent a year if bought through a broker. The competition and regulatory scrutiny have resulted in a cut in fees and very low-cost index funds by large investment firms such as Fidelity, Vanguard, and TIAA-CREFF.

Disadvantages[7]

- May have a limited enrollment period;

- May significantly reduce opportunities for financial aid;

- Does have limited participation. Only certain schools participate; and

- May not cover some costs. If child attends an out-of-plan school, some costs may not be covered.

Custodial Accounts (UGMAs and UTMAs)

A custodial account is established for the benefit of a minor child and managed by the parent or other custodian. The custodian controls the account until the child reaches the age of majority. However, unlike the 529 savings plan or ESA account, the child is the legal owner of the account. The account is established at a bank or other financial institution under a state's UGMA or UTMA account.

Advantages

- The custodian controls the account until the child reaches majority age and can use it to pay for any reasonable expense incurred by the child;

- Any contribution to the account is part of the annual $12,000 gift tax limit for an individual and $24,000 for both parents. Grandparents, relatives, or friends can contribute to the account;

- Although the types of investments permitted vary by state, cash, real estate, securities, and life insurance may be allowed; and

- These plans are fairly easy to open, maintain, and have lower costs than a trust.

Disadvantages

- Child takes control of the money at the age of majority (ages 18 or 21, depending on the state in which you live);

- All income is taxed to the child every year with taxes that are based on whether the child is under or over the age of 14;

- For financial aid purposes, more of the money is counted toward the EFC;

- Gifts made to UTMA/UGMA accounts are irrevocable; and

- Accounts must be terminated once the child reaches the age of majority.

Questions to Answer Before Choosing a Plan

Do You Want To Exercise Control over the Account Rather than Relinquish Control to Your Child?

Financial aid calculations by organizations all assume that the person getting the education should pay the lion's share of the expense of a college education. Parents are certainly concerned about handing over control of their well-earned income for fear that the money could be spent on a new car or Caribbean vacation. The 529 savings account, ESAs, and mutual funds owned by parents are considered parental assets. Retirement accounts such as pension plans, IRAs, and Roth IRAs (but not distributions from the

Roth) are not part of financial aid formulas. Any 529 savings accounts held by grandparents or other relatives do not figure in financial aid formulas. Custodial accounts such as UGMAs or UTMAs are considered to be the student's assets. Any transfers from a 529 savings account to a UGMA or UTMA are similarly part of the student's assets.

Many investment advisors suggest that parents should save money in their own names and control their assets if they: are not sure if the child will go to college; want to keep the assets out of the child's name for financial aid reasons; wish to minimize the cost of a separate account or trust; and want to have maximum investment flexibility. Of course, this option will have tax consequences depending on your tax bracket.

What Is Your Time Horizon?

The time horizon is an important consideration in picking the appropriate plan for your child. If you have started saving recently for your child who is college-bound soon, the best fit may be a 529 college savings plan, a UGMA, or a UTMA plan because these allow the largest contributions in the least amount of time. If you have a preschool child, all of the options are available. You can contribute to both an ESA and a 529 plan.

Do You Want To Contribute More than or Less than $2,000 a Year?

You can only contribute up to $2,000 per beneficiary under an ESA account. The limit is much higher for 529 savings plans, as mentioned.

Would You Trade Flexibility for Tax-Deferred or Tax-Free Growth?

On the one side, there is the flexibility to use the funds for any purpose to benefit the child via an UGMA arrangement vs. the tax-advantaged growth of a "qualified educational expense" (529) savings plan. For most parents, the tax-free growth and potential federal tax-free distribution characteristics of the 529 college savings plans and ESAs may be the most attractive alternatives. Also consider the fact that a tax-free gift (up to the annual gift tax limit) can be contributed to both of the plans in the same year.

Is It Important that the Percent of the Account's Value Be Minimized So That It Doesn't Count Against Financial Eligibility?

Student assets such as UTMA/UGMA plans result in greater reduction in financial aid in contrast to ESA and 529 plans.

Important Tips for Funding Higher Education

Keep the following in mind when considering higher-education matters:

1. Keep a list of all the deadlines for filing applications;

2. Submit the financial aid information as soon as you can after January 1 preceding the student's freshman year;

3. Don't rule out expensive private colleges. Parents of gifted students with meager savings may be discouraging them from applying to expensive private colleges. However, the same private colleges may have the endowments to subsidize gifted students. In the annual *U.S. News & World Report* on best colleges, the largesse of the college can be gauged by a review of the average discount and the percent of undergraduates receiving grants meeting financial need.[8] If the college is over 50 percent in both categories, there is a good chance for your child;

4. Look to federal programs first if your child must borrow. Both the Perkins and the subsidized Stafford loans have reasonably low interest rates (5 percent and 6.8 percent, respectively, on July 1, 2006) and the interest is due only after graduation;

5. Check with your financial advisor before borrowing from either a traditional or Roth IRA. Even though you can tap into these funds, it may not be a good idea. First, you will pay taxes on withdrawal from a regular IRA. In addition, the distributions from a Roth IRA may be considered as income for the next year's EFC;

6. Retain control of funds in savings plans. Although financial aid may not be an option for many high-income earners, financial aid formulas do change over time. Because the current stance on federal aid is that students are expected to be the largest contributors to their educational expense, it may make sense for parents to retain control of the funds placed in 529 plans and prepaid tuition plans;

7. Watch for front-load and high annual fees for plans such as the 529 plans sold by some brokers; and

8. Keep abreast of changes in pension and tax laws. Congress passed the Pension Protection Act of 2006 in August 2006, which was signed by President Bush. The 529 tax permanency provision removes the sunset provision (after 2010) of the tax benefits of 529 plans. The act does not help ESAs, which will still face a 2010 sunset of tax benefits.

Taking these steps will ease your planning efforts as you consider higher-education options for your children.

References

1. The College Board, "Trends in College Pricing: 2005–2006," www.collegeboard.com/prod_downloads/press/cost05/ trends_college_pricing_05.pdf (accessed Oct. 9, 2006).

2. "Private Scholarships Count," Report by the Institute for Higher Education Policy, May 2005, www.ihep.org/Pubs/PDF/ privatescholarshipscount.pdf (accessed Oct. 9, 2006).

3. "35th Annual Survey Report on State-Sponsored Student Financial Aid," 2003–2004 Academic Year, National Association of State Student Grant and Aid Programs, (May 23, 2005), www.nassgap.org/survey/ NASSGAP_Survey_Instrument_2003-04.pdf (accessed April 30, 2007).

4. Fidelity Investments, "Fidelity Poll Shows New Pension Law Could Significantly Increase National Adoption of 529 Plans" News Release (Oct. 2, 2006), http://content.members.fidelity.com/Inside_Fidelity/ fullStory/1,,7229,00.html (accessed April 30, 2007).

5. S. Stevens, "A Crash Course in College Savings Plans," http:// finance.yahoo.com/retirement/saving_for_college/article/101867/ A_Crash_Course_in_College_Savings_Plans (accessed Oct. 9, 2006).

6. K. Greene, "How to Build College Savings for Your Grandchildren," *Wall Street J*, Oct. 7–8 (2006): B4.

7. "Improving Your Retirement: Your Guide to College Savings Plans," column, *Morningstar* (June 29, 2006), www.morningstar.com.

8. D. Weliver, "10 Things College Financial Aid Offices Will Not Tell You," Yahoo.com, (Originally published Jan. 14, 2004 on morningstar.com. Updated Aug. 5, 2005), http://finance.yahoo.com/retirement/ saving_for_college/article/101884/10_Things_College_Financial_Aid_ Offices_Wont_Tell_You (accessed Oct. 9, 2006).

Additional Resources

American Federation of Teachers—aft.org

The College Board—www.collegeboard.com

Morningstar—www.morningstar.com

Saving for College—www.savingforcollege.com

Utah Educational Savings Plan—www.uesp.org

Disclaimer: This chapter is a brief summary of educational savings plans and is not a substitute for comprehensive, expert advice. Tax and legal advisors should be consulted for the most appropriate plan. Each state has different regulations that govern education savings accounts.

Chapter 10

Managing Your Time, Your Career, and Your Life

For many physicians, the following comments are all too familiar:

- "I know how I want to live but cannot make it happen."

- "I don't have enough hours in the day."

- "It's no fun being a physician anymore."

Several surveys have suggested that levels of professional satisfaction among physicians have declined significantly during the past decade. Previous studies had shown about 15 percent of physicians doubted their career choice; more recently, that percentage has climbed to between 30 percent and 40 percent. In querying 2,000 physicians in 1995, 40 percent said they would not recommend the profession of medicine to a qualified college student.[1] The discontent is particularly high among physicians between 50 years and 65 years of age who make up about 38 percent of the nation's practicing physicians. In a survey of these physicians in 2004, the discontent was reflected in the following responses:[2]

- Three out of four (76 percent) said medical practice was less satisfying in the past 5 years (compared with 54 percent in 2000);

- Malpractice worries were the single most-cited source of professional frustration;

- More than half (51 percent) indicated they were going to make a change. Of those, 21 percent planned to retire, take a non-clinical job, or a job outside of medicine in the next 3 years;

- More than half (52 percent) indicated they would not choose medicine if they were just starting to choose a career; and

- Almost two-thirds (64 percent) would not encourage their children or younger people to choose medicine as a career.

It may be no surprise that physician morale is low. Every day brings more depressing news. One day the Medicare program cuts another 4 percent of its physician professional fees. The next day malpractice premiums go up another 10 percent. You or close colleagues may have just received a "180-day" letter about a potential malpractice claim. The hospital may be threatening to suspend your privileges because of incomplete medical records. It seems like you never have enough time to do anything else but work. And there will likely be personal challenges as well: perhaps your daughter is not doing well in school, or your husband has a health problem requiring him to cut back work.

Of course, you would be having a patch of bad luck to have all these things happen in a short span of time. But sometimes events happen quickly, and it may seem like your life is being torn apart while everyone else's life is just fine. In weeks like that, it may be worthwhile to go back to your inner core for sustenance and recovery.

This chapter is about how to keep the inner core alive so it can sustain you during hard times. It all starts with putting your career in perspective as just one facet in a larger context that includes your very existence.

Your Personal Mission and Vision Statements

The entire framework of putting your life and career in perspective starts with a mission statement. The mission statement should be a clear representation of your purpose for existence. When I have asked other physicians if they have a mission statement, there are two responses: (1) it was something they may have done in school or college and never looked at again; or (2) they were aware that organizations had mission statements but not individuals.

Why do businesses have mission statements but individuals are not expected to have them? Is it because in many organizations the statement is put out almost for show, so employees and visitors can be impressed, and thus individuals don't see the need to demonstrate their mission to others? It is possible that physicians have simply moved from striving to reach one demanding finish line and then the next but have never been encouraged, or felt they had a reason, to reflect and write a personal mission statement.

A personal mission statement is about the individual and for the individual. The mission statement is specific, short, plainly worded, and sharply focused. Here are some examples of successful organizations that have simple but powerful mission statements:

- **Avis:** "We try harder;"

- **Sony:** "Our mission is to experience the joy of advancing and applying technology for the benefit of the public;"

- **Coca Cola:** "The basic proposition of our business is simple, solid and timeless. When we bring refreshment, value, joy and fun to our stakeholders, then we successfully nurture and protect our brands;"

- **3M:** "To solve unsolved problems innovatively;" and
- **Cleveland Clinic:** "The mission of The Cleveland Clinic is to provide compassionate health care of the highest quality in a setting of education and research."

Construction of the Mission Statement

List the most important things that really matter to you, the main roles you have, the long-term goals you would like to achieve, and the contributions you would like to leave behind. Paul Beeston states: "To live your mission is the most generous thing you can do. Your mission is always going to make a major contribution to your life, the lives of others and the planet. Humankind and the planet need you to live your mission. Your mission is part of the tapestry of life and without it there are stitches missing. Is there anything more important for you to do?"[3]

Questions to ask yourself before writing a mission statement are:

- What do I care about the most?
- Whom do I care about?
- What do I want to accomplish and why?

An example of a personal mission statement is:

—To remember my Creator at all times, and know that I will have to answer for all my actions and deeds in this life;

—To recognize that my potential for personal growth is infinite;

—To lead my life so my family can remember me as an honest human being, who was trustworthy in marriage, who cared for them deeply, and left a legacy of love and core values to be passed on;

—I will value loyalty, treat friends and co-workers with dignity, be tolerant, and strive to remain humble;

—To be a model of professional integrity and have my patients say that I cared;

—To try and maintain a sense of humor, know that perpetual happiness in life was not guaranteed at birth, and remember that the bad days shall pass.

Construction of a Vision Statement

A mission statement is often confused with a vision statement. The vision statement describes how you see yourself in the future and the mission statement describes how you will get there. A mission statement may define the bigger goals and is a guide for your actions with essentially no time frame. If a mission statement defines how you will achieve your goals, a vision statement defines what your success will look like. It graphically portrays what the future will look like.

It is widely accepted that you will never be greater than the vision you have of yourself. The vision statement should require an individual to go beyond expectation, aspiration, or performance. A vision statement should identify the direction and purpose of your life and paint a picture in concrete terms of what your life will look like years from now. It needs to be a beacon, especially during dark days when you need to remind yourself of what you have seen for yourself. A vision statement can be a few words or several pages. For individuals, a paragraph or two should capture the essence of the future a person wants to be a part of. If a person, organization, or business wishes to be a world-class entity, then its vision statement must paint a picture of what it must look like.

Before you start on a vision statement you may wish to consider:

- What are your most important core values? Is it your faith, your family, your vows?

- What makes you feel fulfilled at the end of the day? Is there one overarching passion?

- What do you need to accomplish to give you the most satisfaction before you die?

Following are examples of organizational vision statements as posted on their Websites in June 2007:

- **Emory University:** "A destination university internationally recognized as an inquiry-driven, ethically engaged, and diverse community, whose members work collaboratively for positive transformation in the world through courageous leadership in teaching, research, scholarship, health care, and social action."

- **Society of Gynecologic Oncologists:** "As medical professionals with a special interest and expertise in gynecologic cancers, we dedicate our work to helping women conquer the cancers unique to them. We uphold the highest standards of quality care, and through research we will forge new and innovative ways to improve the treatment and care of our patients. We advocate and contribute to a comprehensive approach to screening, diagnosis and treatment. And we will empower women with knowledge that provides answers, support and hope."

- **Johnson & Johnson:** "We are committed to making Johnson & Johnson the world leader in health and safety by achieving healthy lifestyles and injury free work places."

- **The Ohio State University:** "The Ohio State University will be recognized worldwide for the quality and impact of its research, teaching, and service. Our students will be able to learn and to advance knowledge in all areas. As a 21st century land-grant university, The Ohio State University will set the standard for the creation and dissemination of knowledge in service to its communities, state, nation, and the world. Our faculty, students, and staff will be among the best in the nation."

Example of a Personal Vision Statement

First and foremost, my vision for the future is to leave my wife financially secure, to help my children realize their goals in life, and give more time to my aging parents. My vision for myself is holistic, with continued purposeful growth in all aspects of my life: occupational, recreational, and spiritual. My business knowledge will best be used to consult with and teach business principles to physicians, surgical residents, and medical students. I would like to set up a nonprofit organization, and raise funds to set up a free medical clinic in the part of the world where I grew up. I envisage growth in the artistic area, with continued music lessons. Spiritual growth has been, and will continue to be, a vital part of my existence. I see the end of life approaching, and hope to reach the finish line well prepared. I am convinced this vision is realistic and, assuming good health, it can be realized.

Managing Your Time

Well–thought out mission and vision statements are important for keeping an individual focused on managing the time required to spend on activities to accomplish all of the goals included in the mission and vision statement. For most physicians, the "urgency mode" is operational throughout the day, every day. In one sense, having urgent tasks on hand all day reinforces the importance of being a physician. A status symbol of being a busy, and therefore, a successful physician becomes something the physician tries to live up to. Some physicians appear lost when five things that are urgent are not happening on a quiet day! The problem is that if urgency becomes the dominant mode, it may hurt relationships, particularly at home. It becomes harder to turn off the urgency switch and get used to the normal pace.

Many books have been written about work–life balance. A practical issue is defining a "balance" for you and your partner. A balance certainly does not mean simply touching all the bases in a neatly drawn grid on a piece of paper. It does not mean allocating 50 percent of the time for work and 50 percent for home. What it does mean is finding the right balance that allows you to stay true to your mission and vision. Part of losing ground in the work area of the balance is poor time management. However much work is valued, for individuals to be successful at work and home, the first item of the workday's agenda is getting home to family at a reasonable hour. Frustration occurs when every workday is prolonged, often due to inefficient work habits.

Reasons for Time Inefficiency[4]

Inefficient individuals may:

- Flit from one activity to another with no prioritization;
- Not know how to say "no";
- React to what is "hot" at the moment;
- Not have a clock in their heads and are easily distracted;
- Not know how to "multitask";
- Not understand how to cut off conversations politely; and
- Delegate poorly.

Overcoming the Time Management Roadblock

To achieve your goals, it is vital that you manage your time efficiently. Here are some recommended methods.

Set goals. Decide what is "mission critical." Write down your goals and subdivide them into "critical," "important," "nice if time available," or "not important to your mission." If the goals are important to you, what do you have to give up? Are these compatible with your mission and vision?

Suppose you have decided that your professional mission (or one aspect) is to do excellent medical research. The issues of pay, geography, weather, and clinical success become much less important.

It is just as important to set goals outside of work as it is at work. Ideally, you should start making a list of things you want to accomplish several years ahead of time. Let's assume you want to learn a musical instrument and start playing golf. Because of the time commitment, gaining musical skills will be easier than becoming a good golfer. It may take one to two hours a week for music lessons and another two to four hours a week at home to practice. If you have small children, however, spending many hours at the golf course may have to wait until your family commitments have waned, or your spouse has agreed to help you with these commitments.

What leads to frustration is putting personal goals off until retirement, and then being unable to achieve them for various reasons. It is easier to deal with work frustrations if you are achieving some personal goals as you go along. Attainment of personal goals is helpful in dealing with work frustrations, as well as creating a positive reminder of your ability to execute your plans.

Establish finite timelines. Set a timeline for tasks at work and at home. The timeline may not work all the time, but it does help prioritize tasks you have in mind. It is worthwhile to take a look at the next day, what is on the schedule, and how you see the priorities unfolding. It is important when reviewing the priorities for the next day to remember that 10 other things will probably happen. You have to maintain a long-term approach to goals and remain mission focused.

Appreciate what you are worth. Set a value on your time. "Until you value yourself, you will not value your time. Until you value your time you will not do anything with it."[5]

List your three most common "time wasters" and do something about them. Some of the most common time wasters we encounter at work are discussed here.

- Returning phone calls or answering messages that are unimportant. Have your staff handle the non-essential calls. There is no reason to return cold calls of any sort;

- Allowing e-mails to clutter up your in-box. It is often a mistake to leave your e-mail on all the time because it creates a compulsion to read them and answer back as soon as you receive the e-mail. At the very least, you should block the pop-up sound that announces a new e-mail. Resist the impulse to check every e-mail that comes in. According to the Pareto Principle, 80 percent will be worthless. Pareto's Principle is named after Vilfredo Pareto (1848–1923), an Italian economist and sociologist, who first discovered and described the "80:20 phenomenon." Block as much of the junk mail as possible, forward e-mails to others who can deal with the issue, and keep replies short;

- Failing to challenge anything that seems a waste of your time. This is especially important if you find yourself serving on a "perpetual" committee. Other than an ad-hoc committee with a well-defined endpoint, committees set up to meet on a regular basis with no end in sight are of dubious value. There is almost nothing that happens in a regular committee that cannot be handled with two minutes of discussion by phone or e-mail. Most committees start meetings 10 minutes late to accommodate latecomers, finish late without the agenda completed, and make few decisions because the person with the authority to do so is likely not there. Another trap to avoid during a meeting is too quickly answering a call for volunteers to serve on yet another sub-committee. Committee meetings are useful, but only when the chairperson has the authority to make a decision that can be carried out instantly. As already mentioned, your time is worth something and unless a meeting truly advances your career and/or an institutional goal, or has to do with critical clinician issues such as patient safety, you are donating valuable time you could spend with your family;

- Not assessing new technologies to determine if they will really save time for you, or just save time for others;

- Overestimating your ability to multitask. Not everyone can take on several projects simultaneously. Unless your multitasking skills have been tried and tested, try not to do several projects at the same time. The evidence suggests that for some, multitasking not only aggravates stress but also impairs productivity and leads to substandard quality of work;[6]

- Failing to force yourself to get back to the task at hand. It is not unusual to start searching the Internet for hotels and end up spending the next 30 minutes on a subspecies of minnows that are now endangered;

- Going through paper mail without a purpose. Go through your mail with the goal of touching each piece of mail only once (the OHIO principle or Only Handle It Once).[7] When it comes to mail, either pitch it, have someone file it, or take action. If under your desk's in-box, there is an additional box where you store mail you may need later, be sure to go through that box every month or two. If you have not had the need to use items by then, you probably will never use them and should, therefore, clean the box out. Save any throw-away journals and read them, if you must, in between patients or while on hold on the phone;

- Not giving away as much of the non-critical work as possible. Delegation is hard because you think you can do it better, or it will take too much time to explain how to do the task. Read "Who's Got the Monkey?"[8]

This article has been one of the *Harvard Business Review's* top best-selling reprints ever. The article's thesis is that managers (most physicians are, in a sense, managers) fail to delegate effectively and actually encourage their subordinates to reverse delegate. The authors state that the task is the monkey, and the goal is to get it off your back. Some symptoms, which most physicians will recognize, are: Letting papers pile up on your desk and e-mails pile up in your in-box without dealing with them quickly; delaying decisions, thus frustrating both your superiors and your subordinates; getting farther behind every day; working late and working weekends. Harrington comments that certain responses actually invite the "monkey" to climb on your back:[9]

- "Monkey" promptly climbs on your back—*Let me think about it and I will get back to you;*

- "Monkey" is crawling up your leg—*Send me a memo on that;*

- "Monkey" is swinging above you—*Just let me know how I can help;* and

- "Monkey" straddles both backs—*I will draw up an initial draft for discussion with you.*

White recommends using a scale to instruct subordinates on tasks.[10] This is similar to a hospital consultation where the admitting physician indicates the extent of the consultant's role by checking a box on the consultation sheet (see Figure 10.1).

Figure 10.1   Decision-to-Action Tool

Pick a response when asked to make a decision or take action on non-urgent matter.

____ Look into this problem. Give me the facts. I will decide what action to take if any.

____ Provide me with the alternatives and the pros and cons for each.

____ I will choose a course of action.

____ Recommend a course of action. I will approve.

____ Decide what to do but delay acting until I approve.

____ Decide what to do, keep me advised, and act unless I say not to.

____ Act. Let me know what happens.

____ Act. Communicate with me only if you fail.

____ Act. No other communication is necessary.

Source: Malcolm White. "Tip of the Day—Management: Accountability and Delegating Scale," Communicat, www.communicat.com.au/tipOfTheDay/index.cfm?tipId=8 (accessed Sept. 1, 2006). Used by permission of Communicat.

Learning to Improve Personal Efficiency Through Observation

One thing that wastes a lot of time is finding something that you need. Despite an extensive filing system at work and home, it is amazing how often you rack your brain for something that should be right in front of you. Is there a way you can cut down physically filing the material? Is it possible to generate an electronic filing system that you can search? Is it possible to subdivide the larger paper files or "de-bulk" them once a year to make it easier to find material? Ask people who are time efficient about what and how they file things.

How do busy academic physicians travel around the country every two weeks, conduct research, write papers, serve on university committees, and take care of patients? Take the time to ask them how they manage to accomplish their mountains of work. A sample questionnaire that helps to discover your own effectiveness profile has been published by Covey.[11] These key ideas are worth considering:

- **Learn to disengage when you are not making progress.** Whether it is an issue or a project, plan to revisit it later;

- **Learn to say no.** Learn to say no or drop something you are currently involved in to take on something new. Saying no is sometimes the hardest thing to do. If the task fits with your goals/mission, then you will have to drop something else to take on the new assignment. "A mission statement helps in deciding when to say yes or no. A mission statement teaches us when to say no and how to say yes. When we have no mission statement, we are pushed and pulled by the demands of life. When we have a mission statement, we can set a steady course;"[4]

- **Break things down into small parts.** A big project is always the victim of procrastination. Do the hard part during a time of high energy rather than late in the evening. Set a deadline for each small part of the work or part of the project to be done. Reward yourself with a day off or something you have been looking forward to when the task is finished; and

- **Make your waiting time productive.** You will spend a lot of time waiting for everything from the car mechanic to the next operation. Arrange access to journals, books, a computer, e-mail, or a list of calls you have to complete. Any work you can complete is less work you take home, or it may mean going home sooner to spend time with your family. Productivity is not simply measured by work done. If your mission and vision statements call for spiritual growth or maintenance of strong family ties, "down" time can be used to fulfill your statements. As an example, Covey recommends turning the radio off while driving to meditate, pray, or whatever you wish to do toward your goal.[4] Praying or meditating is not a slave to a time of day. Five minutes of mental tuning out can be refreshing. He also advocates using the time to call relatives or friends on a regular basis to catch up on events.

Gaining and Keeping Balance

Even if you achieve balance between home and work does not mean you can do it all or have everything you wish at your feet. It just means that you have a better chance at staying true to your goals in life. For some, long hours at work are stressful and a source of constant tension at home. For others, not working is stressful and filled with guilt. Why the difference? Some physicians like to work and do not see it as stress (others have referred to them as "happy workaholics").[12] Guilt is often a factor if you are not able to achieve your goal because you did not give it your full effort.

Three factors have been traditionally identified as important for physician satisfaction: autonomy, income, and leisure. With stagnant or negative growth in income, decreased autonomy due to managed care and governmental mandates, leisure has become a decidedly important determining factor in choosing a satisfying career in medicine. The balance between work and leisure may be affected by specialty and gender.

The Influence of Medical Specialty

In a 2004 survey of Canadian physicians regarding balancing professional and personal lives, some specialties such as cardiology, urology, and radiation oncology—which are perceived as having better lifestyles than others—were actually among the least satisfied physician groups.[13] The most satisfied groups were in physical medicine, ophthalmology, psychiatry, dermatology, and radiology. A 1990 study defined 16 specialties as *controllable* (allowing more personal free time for leisure) or *uncontrollable* (little free time).[14] Experts today still use these definitions when discussing work–life issues in medicine and when classifying specialties, as follows:

- **Controllable:** Anesthesiology, dermatology, diagnostic radiology, emergency medicine, neurology, ophthalmology, otolaryngology, pathology, and psychiatry;

- **Uncontrollable:** Family medicine, internal medicine, general surgery, obstetrics and gynecology, orthopedic surgery, pediatrics, and urology.

Gender and Choice of Specialty

Traditionally, the tough choices have been and are mostly made by women physicians in their roles as wives/mothers and career physicians. However, more male physicians are starting to make lifestyle choices that critically evaluate what specialty they will enter. In a survey of 1996–2003 graduating medical students, the percentage of women choosing specialties with controllable lifestyles increased from 18 percent in 1996 to 36 percent in 2003.[15] For men, the percentage grew from 28 percent to 45 percent. In addition, the number of women pursuing controllable lifestyle careers such as anesthesiology, emergency medicine, ophthalmology, psychiatry, and radiology increased by 18 percent. The number of men picking similar career fields increased by 17 percent during the same time period. Men and women both had a declining interest in specialties in which they did not have a work–life balance, such as family medicine. In 1995, 18.9 percent of women and 15.2 percent of men graduating from U.S. medical schools chose family medicine residencies. Eight years later, in 2003, only 10 percent of women and 6.1 percent of men wanted to pursue family medicine careers. The new generation of physicians, the Generation X-ers (born 1965–1980) and the Generation Y-ers (1981–2000), appear to have thought about their vision for themselves and are certainly showing their preference for a balance between work and leisure. It may mean more satisfying careers than the current physician surveys seem to suggest.

Setting Your Own Course for Success

As you define your success, remember to keep in mind these factors:

- Always stay true to your mission and vision statements;

- Use visual reminders. You may not remember your mission and vision statements every day. Therefore, a constant reminder is necessary in the form of a poster, desktop background, a screensaver, or simply a piece of paper in a constant spot on your desk;

- Manage your time efficiently and effectively;

- Maintain a good support system;

- Seek professional help (a personal coach or a counselor) if necessary;

- Take your days off;

- Remember that things on your to-do list are not always going to get done that day;

- Try to talk about things other than medicine when you are with family and friends;

- Ask how you want to use your time. If anything comes up to delay your return home and you have a choice to stay or not, ask yourself: is it worth my time away from home?

- Derive strength from your patients. Get to know them and their stories. They will end up giving you more than you give them;

- Remember why you chose a medical career. The choice of medicine as a career is perforce tied to helping human beings. The satisfaction from helping the sick has not yet been "cut back," despite all the machinations by some insurance companies and plaintiff attorneys; and

- Define success for you.

A key to defining your success is to first come up with mission and vision statements. Then measure success based on how much you have achieved in fulfilling both your mission and vision. The unit by which success is measured is set by the individual, not others. To some physicians, success may mean having the busiest practice or winning the Nobel Prize in medicine. For others, it may be measured by being adored by their patients. Whatever gauge you use, your success should be measured by the extent to which you have achieved your vision and accomplished your mission.

References

1. A. Zuger, "Dissatisfaction with Medical Practice," *N Engl J Med*, 350 (2004): 69–75.

2. Merritt Hawkins & Associates, "Survey Report, 2004 Survey of Physicians 50–65 Years of Age, Based on 2003 Data," merritthawkins.com, www.merritthawkins.com/pdf/2004_physician50_survey.pdf (accessed July 25, 2006).

3. Mission Coach, Change in Mind Ltd., www.mission-coach.co.uk (accessed Sept. 2, 2006).

4. S.R. Covey, A.R. Merrill, and R.R. Merrill, *First Things First*, New York: Franklin Covey Co. (1994).

5. B. Harrington, "Management Time," Aug. 3, 1999, Uniformed Services Academy of Family Physicians, www.usafp.org/Fac_Dev/Leadership_Management/Management%20Skills/Management-Time-and-the-Monkey.html (accessed Sept. 1, 2006).

6. J. Davidson, "Why Multitasking Backfires," *Association Now*, 2 (5) (2006): 14.

7. J.P Kotter, *The General Managers*, New York: Free Press (1982).

8. W. Oncken and D. Wass, "Management Time: Who's Got the Monkey?" *Harv Bus Rev*, November–December (1974): 75–80.

9. B. Harrington, "Management Time," Aug. 3, 1999, Uniformed Services Academy of Family Physicians, www.usafp.org/Fac_Dev/Leadership_Management/Management%20Skills/Management-Time-and-the-Monkey.html (accessed Sept. 1, 2006).

10. Communicat, "Tip of the Day—Management: Accountability and Delegating Scale," www.communicat.com.au/tipOfTheDay/index.cfm?tipId=8 (accessed Sept. 1, 2006).

11. "Seven Habits Profile Habits of Effectiveness," www.franklincovey.com/fc/library_and_resources/self_scoring_7_habits_personal_feedback (accessed Sept. 2, 2006).

12. K.H. Hammonds, "Balance Is Bunk," Fast Company, Oct. 2004, 68. www.fastcompany.com/magazine/87/balance-1.html (accessed Sept. 2, 2006).

13. M.O. Baerlocher, "Happy Doctors? Balancing Professional and Personal Commitments," *Can Med Assc J*, 174 (8) (2006): 1070.

14. R.W. Schwartz and others, "The Controllable Lifestyle Factor and Students' Attitudes about Specialty Selection," *Acad Med*, 65 (3) (1990): 207–210.

15. E.M. Lambert and E.M. Holmboe, "The Relationship Between Specialty Choice and Gender of U.S. Medical Students, 1990–2003," *Acad Med*, 80 (9) (2005): 791–796.

About the Author

Bhagwan Satiani, MD, MBA, FACS, is a professor of clinical surgery in the Division of Vascular Surgery, and medical director of the Non-Invasive Vascular Laboratory at The Ohio State University College of Medicine in Columbus. He is also president of Savvy Medicine, a physician-led organization that educates health care practitioners on business-related topics. He has practiced vascular surgery since 1978. Dr. Satiani's additional professional interests include coordinating business education seminars for physicians and practice management seminars for surgical residents. He also developed an 18-month curriculum for surgical residents in the Department of Surgery to prepare them for the economic, legal, and personal finance challenges ahead of them. Married for 36 years and the father of two children, Dr. Satiani's numerous community interests include volunteering for ASHA—Ray of Hope, a Columbus, Ohio organization to prevent domestic violence in South Asians. He also plays percussion in an Indian music group in Columbus.

About the Contributors

Scot C. Crow, JD, LLM, CFP, is with Roetzel & Andress, LPA, in Columbus, Ohio. (Chapter 7: Estate Planning Essentials: Protecting Your Family and Your Legacy)

John E. Sestina, CFP, ChFC, is president of John E. Sestina & Company, in Columbus, Ohio. (Chapter 2: Investments: What You Need to Know About Stocks and Mutual Funds)

Index